The Creative Writer

Level Two: Growing Your Craft

Publisher's Cataloging-In-Publication Data

Fishman, Boris, 1979–
    The creative writer. Level two, Growing your craft / by Boris Fishman.
    p. : ill. ; cm.
    "… designed to be used in a mentor/student relationship, with teaching,
    guidance, and evaluation tips provided for the mentor or teacher."
—Publisher's e-mail communication.
    Interest grade level: 5-8.
    ISBN: 978-1-933339-56-6

    1. Creative writing (Elementary education)
    2. Creative writing (Middle school)
    3. English language--Composition and exercises--Study and teaching (Elementary)
    4. English language--Composition and exercises--Study and teaching (Middle school)
    I. Title.
    II. Title: Growing your craft

LB1576 .F57 2012
372.62/3   2012931274

For a complete list of history, grammar, reading, and writing materials produced by Peace Hill Press, or to request a catalog, visit **peacehillpress.com**.

The Creative Writer

Level Two: Growing Your Craft

by Boris Fishman

PEACE HILL PRESS
CHARLES CITY, VA

INTRODUCTION

TO THE STUDENT

This is the second volume in a four-volume series. The previous volume, *The Creative Writer, Level One: Five Finger Exercises*, introduced beginning writers to some of the basics of storytelling: plot, character, dialogue. Are you a beginner? Then you may want to pick up that volume instead.

The exercises in this volume refresh and build on the lessons of *Level One*, but stand alone as well. So if you've tried your hand at some poems and short stories, and you read both fiction and poetry for pleasure, and the words "plot" or "dialogue" aren't foreign to you, feel free to start here. You can always backtrack.

This 36-week syllabus is divided into two parts: Fiction and Poetry. The first 18 weeks will focus on fiction, the remaining 18 on poetry. We will concentrate on fundamentals: What makes a short story a short story? How does an author capture the reader's attention and make him or her turn the page? *Why* is it *critical* to capture a reader's attention? But we will also step away from craft guidance to talk about *how writers think*. How should, say, a poet *pay attention to things* in order to come up with descriptions that might make for good poetry? Where do ideas for stories come from? And so on.

FICTION
The 5 Essentials

Some friends of mine have a 7-year-old daughter named Phoebe. Phoebe loves to write short stories. Asked to describe what makes a good short story, Phoebe said: "All you need are some people you care about and the problem they're going to solve." Mark Twain couldn't have put it better. Another way of making Phoebe's point is to say that every story needs a **plot** and **characters**: Something that happens and someone involved in the action.

Unless you're writing a story in which every character is mute or for some reason communicates only by gesture (which would be kind of interesting, actually), your story will also need **dialogue**.

You'll also need to figure out from whose **point of view** you're going to tell the story. Will it be told by a third-person narrator who isn't part of the story or by one of the characters? Will the narrator be able to climb inside every character's thoughts, or will he be able to speak accurately only about his own?

Finally, your story will have to take place somewhere, won't it? Not all stories have an obvious **setting**—sometimes, not having a detailed setting is the author's way of indicating that the characters and story are meant to be universal—but this year, ours will.

There you have what might be called The 5 Essential Ingredients of a traditional short story. You can write a good short story without including every one of them, but first you must master the writing of short stories that include them. That will be our goal this year.

As you'll see in the table of contents that follows, we'll start each unit by focusing on one of the 5 Essentials, using the same short story each time, a fairy tale by the Brothers Grimm. If you think you're too old to use fairy tales to learn about creative writing, think again. In our time, "fairy tales" may be for children, but fairy tales like "Rapunzel" and "The Golden Goose" (this year's selection) are rarely the simple, sugary delights we think of as "fairy tales." The first editions of the Grimms' fairy tales, actually, were criticized because so much of the contents was deemed unsuitable for children by the reading public. So, think of these fairy tales as the *E.T.* and *Star Wars* of the 18th and 19th centuries: serious entertainment for kids and adults alike. (I guess that would make the Grimms the Steven Spielberg and George Lucas of their era.) These stories have endured for a reason: though they were written hundreds of years ago, they continue to make sense for our lives today.

What's more, such fairy tales make for excellent study of creative writing basics like plot. A lot of these stories originated as oral folktales—that is, people told them to each other; the Grimms were, in fact, the first to collect them in a printed edition—and as anyone who has ever told a story or a joke knows, the first rule of story-telling is: You have to keep the audience's attention. There are many ways to do this, but the most obvious is to *get your listeners interested in what happens next.* I emphasize those words because you will be hearing them a lot in the course of this year's study. Here we'll remember Phoebe, our 7-year-old guide: If the characters in a story are interesting for one reason or another, the reader will want to know what happens to them. And if these characters find themselves in a situation whose outcome is unclear—like any good movie cliffhanger—it's a good bet readers will be at the edge of their seats, wanting to find out how the story ends.

When I started writing, it never occurred to me to think about my audience—that is, what would make the story interesting to *my readers.* And yet, if you asked me for whom I was writing, I'd say: an audience. I wasn't writing for my "desk drawer," so to speak; I wanted people to read my stories. And yet, I gave zero thought to what would make the stories interesting for *them* to read. Believe it or not, the random workings of our minds are not automatically interesting to other people, even if our stories are smart or well-written. More than intelligence and beautiful language is required if a piece of writing is to be called great *fiction.* Intelligent, original writing is good *writing*; intelligent, original storytelling is good *fiction.* That's what we're going to practice *a lot* in the fiction section: how to tell a *story.* The good news is: You already know how to do it. It isn't that different from the way you tell a story in ordinary life, or the way you time a joke. So you're halfway there.

POETRY
The 5 Essentials

Just like fiction, poetry can be said to have a handful of essentials. And as with fiction, five essentials help answer the question: What makes a poem a poem? You can probably guess several of them already. For instance, what do many poems have in common, something that immediately distinguishes them from short stories?

For one thing, poems use incomplete lines that "break" well before they've reached the right margin of the page. So, **line breaks** are an essential aspect of poetry.

As you must already know from your study of poetry in English class, many poems **rhyme.** This is especially true of older poetry. Modern poetry rhymes a lot less frequently. Instead, contemporary poems use what's known as *free verse*; that is, verse that doesn't rhyme.

What else makes poetry unique? If you've studied any Shakespeare, you know that he often used something called iambic pentameter. This term refers to the rhythm created by the words in a line of poetry. In this case, "iambic" means that unstressed and stressed syllables will alternate. That probably sounds confusing, but all that "stress" refers to is which syllable gets an accent when we pronounce a word. Think of a word like "bouquet." We say bou-QUET, not BOU-quet, right? That is, we stress the second syllable, not the first. There are variations on this rule, but that's the basis of it.

And "pentameter" (from the Greek *pent-* or *penta-*, which means "five") means that a line will have five such unstressed-stressed combinations. A more playful way of putting it would be to say that a line of iambic pentameter sounds like this: da-DUM da-DUM da-DUM da-DUM da-DUM.

The rhythmic structure of a poem is known as **meter**. Just like rhyme, strict meter is more common among older poems. But even contemporary poems use meter to some extent. In either case, it will be useful to learn how it works, because meter contributes so much to how a poem sounds. We'll begin to this year.

Which brings us to the next essential aspect of poetry, one that arguably takes in both rhyme and meter: **sound**. Sound is important in short stories, too, but because poems use far fewer words than stories, it's that much more important in poetry. Sound in poetry takes many different forms—rhyme, meter, repetition, other kinds of patterning—and is something we will explore across different lessons this year.

Also, we will discuss **how to decide what to write about**, as well as spend several lessons talking about **word choice**. That is, we will practice finding the ideal word for a line of poetry, individual word choice being that much more critical in a poem because of the far fewer words it uses. We're going to get up close and personal with words to see what they're made of.

But perhaps even more important, the longest unit this year will cast aside all this dutiful craft study and focus on *nonsense*. That's right. We're going to practice making as little sense as possible in our poetry. Why? Because poetry is about more than literal meaning. It's about sound, and conveying a certain feeling or mood. Very often, conjuring these sensations has nothing to do with what the poem *means*. In fact, meaning can get in the way! We will explore this mysterious notion together this year.

IN CLOSING

Before we move forward, one final but critical note: Creative writing isn't a science. Even though I talk about "rules," a more accurate term might be "guidelines." Unlike math, creative writing has no formulas. Anything goes, as long as you can make it original, interesting, and all the other qualities of good fiction and poetry. The best thing you can do for yourself as you begin this year's exercises is to discard the idea that there's an absolute right or wrong answer in most of the situations we will encounter along the way.

So, my challenge to you in the following pages is to not worry about "the right answer." Initially, all my talk about craft may sound like there are very specific ways to write. But that would misrepresent my point. As with so many things in life, the best writing comes from something a wise person once called "disciplined abandon"—that is, go wild, but help harness and shape your energy and talent with creative restrictions. How can restrictions be creative? This year's syllabus tries to answer that question.

TABLE OF CONTENTS

Fiction

FICTION SECTION I • PLOT

FICTION SECTION 2 • CHARACTER

FICTION SECTION 3 • DIALOGUE

FICTION SECTION 4 • SETTING

FICTION SECTION 5 • POINT OF VIEW

FICTION SECTION 6 • STORY UNIT: THE SCENE

FICTION SECTION 7 • STORY UNIT: WRITE A SHORT STORY

Poetry

POETRY SECTION I • WHAT TO WRITE ABOUT?

POETRY SECTION 2 • WORD CHOICE

POETRY SECTION 3 • FORM AND SOUND

POETRY SECTION 4 • NONSENSE

POETRY SECTION 5 • WRITE A POEM

FICTION

PLOT

PLOT

Purpose: To examine how plot works in a short story.

Authors of fiction have different opinions about how much to plan before sitting down to write. Some authors don't plan at all, except for having a general idea and maybe the first sentence. Others come up with major plot points, and fill in the details as they go. Still others plot out every little thing in advance.

Different approaches work better for different authors. Generally speaking, the last of the three can be confining. If you plan out every detail in advance, you give your story little opportunity to "surprise" you. When we start writing, all sorts of unexpected things happen. For instance, a character we had planned on making minor might start speaking in such an infectiously funny voice that we realize we have to award them a larger role in the story. But if it was part of our "plan" to kill them off within two pages, that plan is pretty limiting, isn't it?

This said, this third approach—plot everything in advance—is a wonderful aid for beginning writers. A story is a scary thing to try to write. Even for seasoned writers, a blank page, whether in a notebook or on the computer, is a small nightmare. There are worse ways to start than by drawing up a 10-point plan to follow. Creating such a 10-point plan for a short story will be Part 2 of your assignment this week. Part 1 will be to read "The Golden Goose," by the Brothers Grimm, in Appendix I and map out what the Grimms' 10-point plan could have been, if they had come up with one.

You may wish to read the story once for information, and then, as you read a second time, to mark each new plot development as you go. In brief, plot points answer the question, "What happened next?" Every time something new happens in the story, that's a plot point. If you can come up with about 10 during your reading, you'll have done Part 1 of your assignment while reading the story!

PART 1

What is the plot of "The Golden Goose"? In other words, what happens in the story?

To make plotting out easier, it may help to divide the story into several sections:

    I. What happens when Dullhead and his brothers go to the forest to chop wood.
   II. The events at the inn where Dullhead goes to spend the night with his goose.
 III. Dullhead's journey toward the town ruled by the king.
 IV. The challenges assigned to Dullhead by the king.

Quite a few things happen in each of these sections, but these are the main "movements," to use a musical term. When thinking about writing a story of your own, it may help, before you begin, to have this kind of general idea of the "movements" in a story. So, going back to "The Golden Goose," **the first part of your exercise this week is to map out a total of 10 connecting details in the "movements" detailed above.**

1. Try to highlight distinct, important plot developments, as opposed to every last detail.

2. If sentences 2 and 3 in a paragraph in the story serve as nothing more than elaborations of sentence 1, don't mention them.

3. Here's a handy guideline: Your plot summary should be detailed enough for someone who has never read the story to learn all its major plot developments. But you should do this in as few entries as possible.

A sample answer is provided below, but don't peek! Remember that your answers don't have to overlap with mine perfectly. Also, the number 10 is somewhat arbitrary. If your plot outline runs over or under by a couple of plot points, that's fine.

Plot points in "The Golden Goose":

I. What happens when Dullhead and his brothers go to the forest to chop wood.
   a.
   b.
   c. (or however many you need)

II. The events at the inn where Dullhead goes to spend the night with his goose.
   …

III. Dullhead's journey toward the town ruled by the king.
   …

IV. The challenges assigned to Dullhead by the king.
   …

PART 2

Part 2 of your exercise is to reverse Part 1. That is, come up with major plot movements for a story idea, and then populate them with 10 (or so) connecting plot points. For that, you'll need some situations or story ideas. If you're stuck, here are a few:

1. A character is spending the summer working in a bookshop. One day, a boy she really likes—not much of a reader, as far as she knows—comes into the store and tries to shoplift a book.

2. The day the president of the country came to town.

3. A young man whose father won't let him sail by himself determines to show his father that he's capable by taking the family boat out by himself in the middle of the night.

So, what you would do, if, say, you chose #1, is start by coming up with the major plot strokes of the story. Three or four should suffice. You can use "The Golden Goose" as a model.

1. Adelaide and Paul live in the same town and their families see each other often, but he hardly notices her.

2. Adelaide takes a job in a bookshop for the summer while Paul joins a lacrosse camp in town.

3. Adelaide's summer

4. Paul walks into Adelaide's bookshop and tries to steal a book.

5. Resolution

Note that these movements don't cover more than the basic directions of the plot. These "stage directions" don't explain everything that will happen—but what does happen should relate to these overarching movements. The next step would be to populate them with plot points, for instance:

1. Adelaide and Paul live in the same town and their families see each other often, but he hardly notices her.
   a. The story opens at a local baseball game (the town hosts a AAA farm team). Many of the town's families are in attendance. We see Paul through Adelaide's eyes. She does several things to see if he'll notice her, but he seems occupied by the game and his friends.
   b. Streaming out of the stadium after the game, Adelaide is shoved by someone rushing out. She assumes it's her little brother, but it's Paul, jostling with his friends.
   c. The weather is finally turning warm in this northern town. Some paragraphs of description of the town, its character, and the season from Adelaide, leading into the second movement.

2. Adelaide takes a job in a bookshop for the summer while Paul joins a lacrosse camp in town.
   …

Note how several new details/concerns crept in as I worked on the plot points: baseball game, the town hosts a farm team, the town is far north, etc. Some of these details may fall away or have to be changed as I work on the actual story, but they provide a wonderful starting point.

Now, you can continue on to creating plot points for the remaining movements of your story.

Before you move on to the challenge exercises, I'd like you to note that there are a lot of things in "The Golden Goose" that don't make sense. For instance, why does Dullhead head to the inn instead of returning home? I suppose it may have been too late to return home, but then why and where does he set off with the goose the next day? His journey makes no sense in the context of the information we've been given. And it's hard for us to believe that he wouldn't trouble

himself "in the least" about all these strange people stuck to his goose. Maybe we're meant to conclude that Dullhead is too simple-minded, kind as he is, to worry about these things, but these unjustified plot points did stick out in my mind. (The last one is an issue more of character than plot.) Were there any other details in the story that didn't make sense to you?

The reason I point this out is to demonstrate that even legendary stories have flaws. A short story, like a poem, remains a work in progress even when the author decides that s/he has "finished" it. Even the best authors and poets take shortcuts, leave things unexplained, or include unrealistic details. They're human beings, they're not perfect, and they're trying to sort out a lot of information at the same time. Short stories and poems can be thought of as complex machines with an extraordinary number of moving parts: An author is simultaneously trying to figure out plot, character, dialogue, etc. He's recreating a whole world from scratch! So it's a small miracle good stories are as good as they are. All of this is to say: Don't be daunted. Even the masters mess up.

CHALLENGE EXERCISES

1. Cross out plot points 6–10 and write a new ending for "The Golden Goose."

2. Imagine that the Grimms never got to write this story. Imagine they got started—"There was once a man who had three sons. The youngest of them was called Dullhead, and was sneered and jeered at and snubbed on every possible opportunity."—and never returned to the story. Come up with a 10-point plot for a story beginning with these sentences that bears no resemblance to "The Golden Goose." Remember that you can set this story in modern times and alter any details in the story. In fact, this challenge exercise requires you to.

In an upcoming lesson, you will practice creating suspense in your stories. Not in the "thriller" sense of "who robbed Columbia Savings Bank?" but in the sense of, "I'm curious to find out how this will resolve itself; that is, what will happen next." Reread "The Golden Goose" and put a checkmark in the margin every time the story does something to make you wonder how things will turn out.

To give you an example, just yesterday I was reading a short story. I thought it was pretty boring. It described the relationship of a man and his wife. Not much happened in the story—just a lot of description of how they met, where they lived, and some special powers the woman possessed. Then the story seemed to settle down into an account of a very harsh winter. So harsh that this couple, who lived in a remote place, couldn't even get out to go to the grocery store for supplies. My attention perked up. I began to wonder how things were going to turn out. Would they make it? The suspense of that was engaging. So, this would have been a spot I would have marked. Noticing our spikes in interest as we read can be difficult—the whole point is that when our interest spikes, we forget we're reading a story and "fall into" the described world—but it's a valuable skill to start practicing, because a good author is always thinking about what's likely to stir his reader's attention.

SUSPENSE

Purpose: To practice creating suspense in plot.

This week, we're going to look more closely at how an author creates suspense in a short story. Creating suspense makes the reader wonder what's going to happen next. What's likely to do that?

There are many answers to that question, but here's the simplest: conflict. Let's say you pick up a short story in which the situation involves an underdog boxer from a down-and-out neighborhood taking on the cocky heavyweight boxing champion of the world. Naturally, we want to find out who's going to triumph in this conflict, so we read on. (Our interest, of course, depends on the characters being engaging. We'll discuss more what that means in the Character section.)

Here's a less literal alternative: Her whole life, Donna has been dreaming of going out-of-state to college. Her parents want her to remain in town. Will she achieve her dream?

What's the difference between the story about the boxers and the story about Donna? In the boxer story, the conflict is between two individuals. In Donna's, it's between Donna and her parents, but it's also between Donna and her dreams. Will Donna get to do what she wants? If we find Donna interesting, we'll want to know.

So, there are different kinds of conflict: You might write about a **literal** conflict between two forces—like two teams or two businesses or two countries, or two animals—or a less literal one, like Donna's above. In this latter type of story, the character tends to be on a **quest**.

In a quest story, what creates suspense is the desire of a character to achieve something in the face of long odds. Let's say a mountaineer is trying to become the first to climb a mountain in conditions no one has attempted before. Or a farmer is trying to grow vegetables at an altitude where no one has succeeded in growing anything but potatoes. Won't you be curious to find out what happens? "Quest" stories are a type of conflict story because what's a quest without something standing in its way? Not very suspenseful! (Think about it: Would you like to read a story about a teenager who decides to have a bake sale to benefit a local library, and the whole town decides to help, and everything turns out hunky-dory? Didn't think so.)

The basic outline of suspense in a story goes like this:

A. Situation
B. Conflict—either **literal** (between two opposing forces) or **quest** (between a character and whatever stands in the way of her goal)
C. Climax
D. Resolution

If you were to represent this sequence as a diagram, it would look like this:

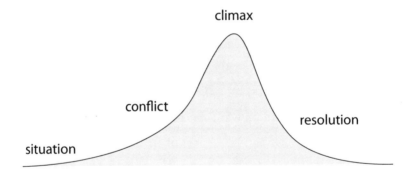

So, to use an example from above:

1. **Situation:** Reinhard Tobolowsky has climbed every mountain in his native Austria except one. To set the record for having climbed all of Austria's peaks in record time, Tobolowsky has to climb the last one this winter. But because he got delayed returning from his last climb, it's fairly late in this season, and he risks getting trapped in a snowstorm.

2. **Conflict:** Will he make it?

3. **Climax:** Up on the mountain, Tobolowsky becomes trapped in a snowstorm. If he keeps going, he may die, though he will die a record holder—but only if he reaches the top.

4. **Resolution:** He pushes on. When he reaches the top, with his last strength, he wedges the poles of his tent as far into the snow as he can, so those who follow can see that he made it. The story ends with Reinhard clinging to life as the snow piles on and his supplies dwindle.

Your assignment this week will be to come up with three situations and trace them through three conflicts, climaxes, and resolutions, respectively. Aim to write about 25–50 words for each of the entries, as above. Make sure that at least one of your conflicts is **literal** and two **quest**, or vice versa.

In coming up with a **situation**, make sure yours answers one of two questions: Is it ripe for conflict? (Literal conflict) Or, does it include a character who wants something she's not sure she can get? (Quest conflict)

Then, the **conflict** becomes easy to figure out: Which of the two parties will come out on top? (Literal conflict) Or, does the character achieve his goal? (Quest conflict)

The **climax** is the moment which will answer these questions.

The **resolution** is what follows, the new order of things established by the resolution of the conflict.

If you're stuck for situations, I mention a couple below. Note that situations hardly have to be grandiose for readers to become interested: A local businessman who opens a restaurant in a "cursed" spot where five previous restaurants have failed is story enough. Also note that conflict doesn't have to be "literal"—a game, a competition, etc. Mom wanting to move homes, and Dad wanting to stay—that's conflict, too. (Note, also, that "conflict," in this sense, doesn't have to be rancorous; it merely refers to two sides with different views.)

More situations:

1. A remote farm has been enduring a record drought. If the rains don't come soon, the crop will wither, and with it, any chance of keeping the operation going. Out wandering one day, Riley, the youngest son, meets a Native American man who says he can direct him to a spring that holds enough water to irrigate the crops of 10 farms like his father's.

2. John is really short, but he's dying to make the basketball team.

3. Every time Mom plants flowers, a deer chews them up.

CHALLENGE EXERCISES

1. An assignment from Janet Burroway's wonderful primer for beginning writers, *Writing Fiction*[1]: Using any one of your situations, write a 100-word short story. Feel free to include dialogue, details on setting, etc. But remember: you have only 100 words. The point of this exercise is to practice the suspense tools listed above (situation, conflict, climax, resolution) in narrative rather than bullet-point form.

2. Watch your favorite television show or movie. Plot out that episode's or film's situation, conflict, climax, and resolution.

---

1 Burroway Janet. *Writing Fiction*. 6th ed. (White Plains, NY: Longman Publishers, 2002.)

STORY FROM A SENTENCE

Purpose: To learn how to develop a story from a first sentence.

"With me, a story usually begins with a single idea or memory or mental picture. The writing of the story is simply a matter of working up to that moment, to explain why it happened or what it caused to follow."

—*William Faulkner*

If you remember, your introduction to plot in Week 1 mentions that different authors approach story planning differently. Some map out the stories in lots of detail in advance. Others come up with only the broad strokes. If the authors of "The Golden Goose" were of this latter group, their planning would sound something like the four "movements" I highlighted in Week 2.

A third set of writers begins a short story with nothing more than a very general idea of what it will be about. For instance, for his story "The Governor's Ball," the short-story writer Ron Carlson knew only that he wanted to write about a mattress flying off the back of a pick-up truck, as he explains in his great how-to-write-a-short-story book *Ron Carlson Writes a Story*. It had happened to him once, it stayed in his memory, and he had come to regard it as one of those strange events that deserves deeper exploration. ("There's something there," such an author might say to himself.)

To figure out the rest of his plot, Carlson didn't open a notebook and begin an outline. He simply started writing. He wrote the first sentence and waited.

"I didn't know until I had the ten-ton wet carpet on top of the hideous load of junk and I was soaked with the dank rust water that the Governor's Ball was that night."[2]

Authors who start with only a general idea will often try to "listen" to the story to figure out where it should go next. They'll put down a single sentence, as Carlson did, and examine its details for suggestions on what might happen next. Notice the emphasis on "might"—there's no law about what a story *must* look like. The same story, on the same subject, can be written an infinite number of ways.

You'll notice that Ron Carlson gave himself a lot of help in that first sentence. What do I mean by this? Well, if his first sentence was "There was a mattress in the back of the truck," it wouldn't be a bad sentence. Immediately, we'd start wondering why it was there. Maybe a couple had a bad argument and one of them was moving out? But you'll agree that there's a lot more **detail** and **specificity** in the sentence with which Carlson starts. Let's look at it more closely.

We guess that it might be raining (the carpet is wet, and the narrator is soaked, too); it sounds like he's in a pretty mean mood ("ten-ton" is obviously an exaggeration, but it gives us a great idea of how carrying the carpet feels to him); and then the big plot-mover: the revelation that there's some kind of ball that evening. Balls are pretty spiffy affairs, so we're hoping the narrator hasn't already changed into a tuxedo, because he's "soaked with the dank rust water." (Come to think of it, putting our main character in a tuxedo that's just been ruined by "dank rust water" wouldn't be bad at all. Anything that places our hero in a predicament and makes the reader wonder how it's all going to turn out means an author has done her job.) Think of all these possibilities as yarns of

2 Carlson, Ron. *Ron Carlson Writes A Story.* (Saint Paul, MN: Graywolf Press, 2007), p. 22. By permission from the author.

string, and yourself as the cat whose job is to unwind them. You don't have to unwind every one, but you want to give yourself a couple of yarns to work with.

Let's look at Carlson's next sentence to see which of his strings he decides to spool out:

> "It was late afternoon and I had wrestled the carpet out of our basement, with all my strength and half my anger, to use it as a cover so that none of the other wet wreckage that our burst pipes had ruined would blow out of the truck onto Twenty-first South as I drove to the dump."

We know that Ron Carlson isn't a planner. So we know that he doesn't know where the story is going to go. But it's no reason to panic. He's given himself a wet carpet in the first sentence. It's all too natural for him to ask himself: How did the carpet get wet? Is it ruined? It must be, if the narrator is throwing it out. Well, how did it get ruined? Did the dog tear it up? But then why is it wet? I've got it (Carlson says to himself)! The pipes burst! Well, what else got wet? I don't have time to think about that now—I'll just say something general like "wet wreckage." Most significantly, Carlson gives the string a little bit more room to unspool when he mentions that his narrator is about to take a ride to the dump. A ride to the dump may not sound like much, but it's actually something that might use a couple of paragraphs of description, and is rife with all sorts of plot opportunities. (Does the narrator get into an accident? Does he take a wrong turn? The possibilities are endless.)

By now, you should be getting a sense of what I mean by "listening" to the story, as this set of authors does. Authors who "listen" to the story will insist that it's the most natural way to write. Come up with a general idea of what it will be about (mattress blows off pickup truck) but nothing more specific, and then pay very close attention to the details. Imagine each word in the sentence as a secret that can give up the goods on where the story should head. This approach forces you to look more closely at the imaginative possibilities of a given word. By "imaginative," I mean that you're not necessarily focusing on its sound, as you might in poetry. You're focusing on every plot direction the word can take you. "Mattress" might take one author to a mattress store, another to a dusty attic, and a third—Ron Carlson—to a pickup slugging across a bridge in Salt Lake City.

The logic of authors like Ron Carlson is understandable. (We touched on this in Week 1.) You might come up with a very nice preplan for this kind of story, they say.

For instance: John has to return a mattress to the store where he and his wife Samantha bought it because it was a cheap mattress and the springs collapsed. When he reaches the store, he learns that the store itself has gone under. In the meantime, Samantha calls in tears because their landlord has evicted them and repossessed their belongings for failing to pay rent. Well, at least we have a mattress to sleep on, John says. End of story.

It's not bad. But by planning nothing more detailed than "John has a mattress in the bed of his pickup," you're leaving yourself open to a lot more possibilities. Imagining the plot points in advance is like practicing football throws before a game. It's useful but it matters a lot more in the game itself. It's only once you're in the game that your imagination is truly engaged. All of a sudden, the story details start sounding less generic and more specific. Trying to imagine—as you're actually writing the story—why John has a mattress in his pickup, you might imagine it's raining or snowing. That, in turn, might remind you of something you noticed last time it was raining or snowing: Cars were fishtailing. You might add this detail to the story. This much snow makes you wonder whether John's truck has all-wheel drive. That makes you wonder whether it's a new or old truck, whether John is poor, whether he is underdressed for the weather. And before you know it, you have a full-fledged character with a style of dress, an income level, and weather with which to struggle. You'll agree it's highly unlikely that you could have thought of this much particular detail if you were trying to map out the story in advance. Planning in advance often forces you to work with generalities and shoehorns you into a plan.

You can help yourself by writing a first sentence jampacked with detail—weather, clothing, setting—or you can, counterintuitively, do the opposite and write a really broad first sentence like "The new family was different" because it holds that many more possibilities. In other words, "Brian Smalera showed up to the paintball game wearing a bow tie" (detailed) will get you started in one direction; "The new family was different" (broad) in another. But both can work. It all depends on what gets you brainstorming more effectively. The key in both cases, however, is that you limit yourself to that first sentence when preparing.

Let's look at the opening lines of five famous novels to see how their authors began:

1. "All happy families are alike; each unhappy family is unhappy in its own way." (Leo Tolstoy, *Anna Karenina*, trans. Richard Pevear and Larissa Volokhonsky.)

2. "This is a tale of a meeting of two lonesome, skinny, fairly old white men on a planet which was dying fast." (Kurt Vonnegut, *Breakfast of Champions*.)

3. "Mr. and Mrs. Dursley, of number four, Privet Drive, were proud to say that they were perfectly normal, thank you very much. They were the last people you'd expect to be involved in anything strange or mysterious, because they just didn't hold with such nonsense." (J. K. Rowling, *Harry Potter and the Sorcerer's Stone*.)

4. "In my younger and more vulnerable years my father gave me some advice that I've been turning over in my mind ever since." (F. Scott Fitzgerald, *The Great Gatsby*.)

5. "I've watched through his eyes, I've listened through his ears, and I tell you he's the one." (Orson Scott Card, *Ender's Game*.)

What do you make of these openings? Which of these opening sentences give out broad information and which choose to rely on detail? For instance, #1 is *very* broad; #2 is more specific. Other authors set up a mystery in the first sentence—to keep their readers in their chairs, but also to give themselves something to unspool in the sentences that follow. "What advice was that?" we wonder as we read #4. "The one for what?" we wonder, reading #5.

You're not required to start with nothing more than a first sentence and a broad idea of what your story will be about, but it is one of your options, and it can be very effective. The stories that come out of it are invariably more surprising (though sometimes a little more chaotic, too), and that's a great way of keeping the reader's attention.

So, this week, we will practice coming up with five sentences to follow the first sentence of a story. Below find five first sentences. You can use them, or come up with your own. For each one, write the next five sentences in a story—or else write five of your own "first sentences," and then follow each one with five more sentences that take each first sentence a little further on. Either way, you should end up with five six-sentence "story openers":

1. The new family was different.

2. It's a well-known fact that thieves read the obituaries to know which houses will be empty during services for the deceased.

3. Molly and Tim loved one another more than anything else in the world, with the exception of their cats. So it was easy for them to join their lives, save for one thing: Their cats hated each other.

4. "Let a couple of pucks slide by you during the game," the man in the straw hat said to the goalie, "and there's a condo in Florida with your name on it."

5. Kenny was older than us, and as sure as a bull, so whatever he told us to do, we listened. We should have known we would pay for it.

This assignment isn't a contrivance to torture you. Very often story ideas occur not as situations, but as sentences, or fragments of sentences, or even single words or images or ideas. It's important to know how to tease out of these cryptic clues the elements of a story. That's what this lesson practices. For this reason, note that the sentences above have varying levels of specificity. An opener like #1 can go in many more directions than, say, #3, which, like Carlson's opening sentence, is pretty specific. This simulates the fact that very often, your attention will snag on something without a conflict or character quest built in. But it will own your attention nonetheless, either because it's a striking image (a thousand sharks circling the contents of a tuna boat that has capsized) or because it's a general subject you'd like to write about (workers' rights). This exercise helps you figure out how to move forward when that happens.

CHALLENGE EXERCISES

1. Come up with a story plan (10 plot points) to follow your six sentences. (You'll have to pick one of the five assignments in the lesson.)

2. Write an actual story based on the first six sentences which you came up with. Length: at least 500 words.

WALKING BACKWARDS

Purpose: To learn how to develop a story from a climax.

Last week, we talked indirectly about how story ideas occur to us. As you may have noticed, they don't come to us in neat situations ripe for conflict. They occur in every which way. Sometimes, we'll walk by a gorgeous little bird and say to ourselves, "There's something special about that bird, the way it flits about and eats all the time." We don't know the name of the bird, but it caught our attention, and we know we would like to include it somehow in a story. But how? It's not exactly a conflict-filled situation or a character with a quest.

So, you go home and start looking up birds on the Internet to see if you can figure out what kind of bird you saw. To your surprise, it seems like you were charmed by a regular old hummingbird. You have heard the name, but have never seen one. You continue researching and learn that humming-birds are the only birds that don't sing. And that's when you land on a new idea for your story: What if you have a boy who is in love with birds but deaf? When he grows up, he can hardly become an ornithologist (someone who studies birds) because studying birdsongs is a huge part of the job. But he can become a hummingbird expert because hummingbirds don't sing! And already, you've got a character for your story. It still isn't a situation—what's the conflict? what's the plot?—but you're on your way.

Another way that stories often occur to us is backwards. That is, we think of the climax—the big bang toward the end of the story where the story is more or less resolved—first. Take Reinhard Tobolowsky, our mountain climber from Week 2. Let's say the story about him originated in your mind as an image of a man on top of a mountain being slowly covered by snow. What happened to bring things to this climax? That's what we're going to practice this week.

Your job is to come up with five climaxes, and then come up with a situation and conflict that might have led to each. If you're stuck, here are some ideas:

1. A young man alone in the desert as a car drives away from him.
2. A young man in the desert as a car drives toward him.
3. The audience in mute shock at something that has just transpired on a community theater stage.
4. A woman returning a gift, still wrapped, to a doorstep, ringing the bell, and disappearing before the door is answered.
5. A man sleeping on the floor of a pizzeria.

In thinking backward, ask yourself, "How might we have gotten here?" Use the clues in front of you. Let's take #1. Ask yourself, "Why is the car driving away from the young man?" Perhaps the story is about the persisting conflict between parents and a son and the parents finally tire so much of the young man's misbehavior that they leave him in the desert for an evening as a disciplinary measure? That's a joke. (Maybe.) What if the young man has lost a bet? Or maybe a young man, tired of getting bullied by bigger boys in town, decided that he would do the one thing that scares him the most, as a way of becoming less fearful?

That last idea sounds like the setup for a story more than the climax: Another way to define it is: The part of the story that gives the reader the tools to understand what the author wanted to say. What happens during this night in the desert? The climax starts to answer questions rather than pose new ones.

Can you do something similar for the other climaxes or one of your own? **Spend anywhere from a sentence to a paragraph on a character and situation that lead up the climaxes in #1–#5.**

CHALLENGE EXERCISE

Come up with more than a situation and conflict for one of the five climaxes. Come up with a 10-point plot outline that includes the climax and then goes on to finish the story through its resolution.

CHARACTER

CHARACTER REFRESHER

Purpose: To improve our understanding of character.

This week, we're going to consider "The Golden Goose" in terms of its characters. **Start by rereading the story in Appendix I.**

First things first: Who are the main characters in this story? Well, Dullhead, certainly. He's the protagonist, the main character, the one whose fate the audience cares about the most.

The quickest way to make an audience care about a character is to give him qualities that make us sympathize with his situation or a challenge he faces. What were those things in "The Golden Goose"?

Dullhead is quite clearly mistreated by his parents. They think of him as the least intelligent of the three brothers. In general, Dullhead "was sneered and jeered at and snubbed on every possible opportunity." His father discourages him from chopping wood in the forest because even his more intelligent brothers couldn't do well with the task, and his mother gives him a less appetizing meal to take with him. I don't know about you, but this made me feel bad for Dullhead. Whether he's very smart or not—and you'll notice the story never claims he's actually very smart, only that he's kinder than his brothers—my sympathies naturally come to rest with him. As soon as I read of his mistreatment, I wanted something nice to happen to him, a kind of revenge on all the people who don't think much of him. Not only did I want something nice to happen to him, I wanted all those mean people to realize that Dullhead deserved better treatment than they had been giving him.

This is an important lesson. When thinking of a main character for your story, you'll have to think about the feelings that character's predicament is likely to inspire in your audience. If your charac-ter is mean to others, you have to realize that it will be a challenge for readers to identify with him, wish him well, and want to turn the page to find out what happens to him next. (Of course, they might want to turn the page in a de-sire for him to get punished.) Read-ers tend to be patient and forgiving; they will often follow and root for a character who's not exactly a saint, but there has to be something about that character that makes them interested in what happens to him next.

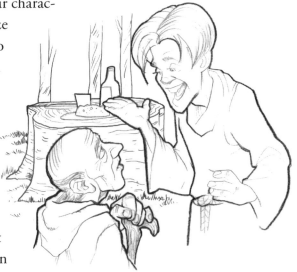

One very easy way to do that is, as discussed, to give this character a quest. Dullhead wants to go into the forest and chop wood, but his parents don't think he's up to it. Dullhead wants the hand of the king's daughter, but the king doesn't want him to have it.

Your job this week is to:

1. List the characters in "The Golden Goose."
2. Figure out whether you like them, dislike them, or feel ambivalence
3. Say why.

Questions you might wish to answer: Do you sympathize with the character? Why or why not? Maybe you do and don't in equal measure? Why? What does the character want? Even if the character is "good," is there anything that makes him or her less than good? If the character is "bad," is there anything that makes him or her not fully bad?

CHALLENGE EXERCISES

1. Come up with 10 character traits for a character an audience will dislike. Don't stop at "he's groggy." Get specific: "He throws his peanut shells on the floor in the restaurant."

2. Do the same things for a character an audience would like.

A CHARACTER WITH WANTS

Purpose: To practice drawing a character on a quest.

I've been saying it over and over: One of the things that makes readers want to read on is a character who wants something she doesn't have and faces an obstacle in acquiring it. The want doesn't have to be monumental—a writer in search of his first published story is suspense enough. Instantly, we become curious whether this individual is going to accomplish her goal. Goals are inherently curiosity-inducing: Is the character going to make it?

Of course, the character in question has to be compelling to us: In one way or another, we have to connect to her, become interested in her. And it's important that the character herself cares about the goal. If she doesn't care whether she gets published or not, we don't much, either. But if she has staked her whole life on it, leaving her job and abandoning her family to shack up in a cabin in the woods ... well, we become curious if the sacrifice was worth it.

Your job will be to come up with 10 characters, the wishes they have, and the things standing in their way. Don't worry, at this point, about characterizing them any further—just focus on detailing their **quest**, as I've been referring to it. Keep in mind that quests don't have to be literal journeys in pursuit of some goal. Wanting to get published is a quest. Wanting Grandpa to feel better is a quest, too.

Here are some examples of what I mean. You'll have to come up with 10 like these:

1. Trudy lives in a rural part of Washington State, where she is destined to remain unless she develops a special skill that makes her a catch for colleges elsewhere. So she begins to run—at first five miles a day, then 10, then 20. The whole story builds up to her tryouts for College X.

Follow your description with a clear breakdown of what's what here:

Character: Trudy

Quest: To escape Washington State

Standing in her way: Tryouts

Suspense: Will she make it out?

2. A dying man decides to drive across the country in blinding winter to visit the last woman he loved. He hasn't seen or spoken to her in 50 years.

Character: Old man

Quest: To find the last woman he loved, 50 years before

Standing in his way: His age, the weather, the question of whether she still lives in the same place or is even alive

Suspense: Will he find her, and what happens when he does?

She wakes up one night to find a talking beaver sitting at her bedside.

3. Zoe Harris's grandfather is ill. She wakes up one night to find a talking beaver sitting at her bedside. The beaver explains that he is the king of the land on which Zoe's family's house sits. Zoe's father might own everything above the ground, but the beaver owns everything beneath it. The beaver's not a great fan of interacting with the humans in the "upperworld," as he calls it, but he understands her grandfather is ill, and there happens to be a plant that grows in the "lowerworld" that might help him. Would Zoe like to come and pick it up? Zoe is suspicious—why couldn't the beaver just bring her the plant?—but she decides to go, anyway.

> **Character:** Zoe
>
> **Quest:** To find the plant that might help her grandfather
>
> **Standing in her way/**
> **Suspense:** Is the beaver telling the truth? If so, will Zoe manage to get the plant?

Now try this for yourself.

Character:

Quest:

Standing in the way:

Suspense:

CHALLENGE EXERCISES

1. Come up with a character on a quest whose obstacle is internal rather than external. For instance, Bobby wants to open a restaurant with the home-nurse who takes care of his grandfather because she's an excellent cook. But doing this—and fulfilling his dream of becoming a restaurant owner—will mean taking the home-nurse away from his grandfather, whom she's kept alive through her care and attention. Bobby's obstacle isn't external; it's his own moral quandary.

2. Pick one of your 10-characters-on-a-quest and flesh out her character; that is, make her interesting to us. (Remember that "interesting" doesn't necessarily mean "saintly.") Come up with a character profile by answering questions about the character: What's likable about her? What's not very likable? Is she kind to strangers or skeptical of them? Why is she on this quest? How will she feel or what will she do if she fails in it?

LET'S FACE IT, WE'RE COMPLICATED

Purpose: To learn how to develop more complicated characters.

What does it mean to develop more complicated characters? As you've heard me say in past weeks, most people in the world aren't only good or bad. They're a little bit of both. Most people mean to do well on most days, but sometimes their impatience or fatigue or envy gets the better of them. While this might make them less than pleasant to be around in real life, this makes them more than pleasant to be around in fiction. Why? Because a goody two-shoes is boring to read about. They're predictable. We know this character will be good and proper in every situation. We can stop reading. There's no suspense there. But with a person who's both intelligent and short-tempered, hard-working but prone to meanness, ambitious but calculating, we are curious to read on and figure out which side of him is going to win out in the situation at hand.

What else might make a character more complicated and lifelike? Something that I introduced in a challenge exercise last week—an obstacle that's internal rather than external. That is, it's easy enough to root for a character working against an easy-to-dislike obstacle. But what if the obstacle is inside oneself? What if achieving the quest means sacrificing some other quest or desire? What if taking care of her grandfather means that Zoe can't go to a better college? To become who she wants to be, Zoe must bear the guilt of abandoning her grandfather—who, say, helped raise her, and for whom there is no one to look after him now, because Zoe's parents are divorced, and her dad is always busy at work? Who does she choose? Her dreams or her family?

Another way to complicate a character is to further push the idea that most people aren't always nice, and make the character shady or even downright unlikable. Take Jack Sparrow in *Pirates of the Caribbean*. He's a pirate. He steals. He keeps getting jailed. In one of the films in the series, he's practically mad, hallucinating a dozen versions of himself. But it goes without saying that we root for him even more than "nicer" characters in the series, like Will Turner, who loves Elizabeth Swann and will do anything to save her in *The Curse of the Black Pearl*. Will is a straight man—necessary, but a little boring. Captain Sparrow is, in the words of the film's director, "dessert."

A different kind of example, from literature: The protagonist of Fyodor Dostoyesvky's *Notes from Underground* is a very difficult man to like or admire. Not because he's evil, because he's petty, sniveling, endlessly self-conscious. But his objection is to a society consumed by self-importance, careerism, and kissing up. We dislike his opponents even more than we dislike him and find ourselves rooting for him. A final example, also from Dostoyevsky, who specialized in complicated characters (though it's a hallmark of any good writer): Raskolnikov, the protagonist of *Crime and Punishment*, becomes so consumed by the idea of justice (and the idea that even murder in the name of justice is forgivable) that he kills an old pawnbroker who benefits from the valuables that poor people like Raskolnikov have to sell in order to get by. Again, Raskolnikov's action is despicable from a moral perspective, but we can't help sympathizing with some of his ideas and his poverty. (And if he is our protagonist—main character—that automatically gets him a lot of our sympathy.) When we read, we don't read from a purely moral perspective.

What about some invented examples? For a character to feel as complicated as real life, we have to feel divided. Let's say we're reading about a college student who gets terrible grades but is a hit with the girls. We know we should dislike him, but we can't help being drawn in by his caddish charm. Or a horse jockey who's mean to his kids but is beautiful to watch on a horse and has won the Kentucky Derby three years running. Those kinds of characters stir complicated feelings—as complicated as life itself.

So, this week, your assignment is to create a complicated character. Your job will be to describe such a character in narrative form for 500 words. Tell us the things that make him/her complicated, of course, but don't stop there. Tell us how he dresses, what she thinks about such-and-such issue, what he likes to eat, whom she was last nice to and whom she was last mean to. You're simply giving us your observations of this person, just in narrative—rather than bullet-point—form.

Where to begin? Make a list of 10 people you know. You can include book characters—think back to the portraits we drew for the main characters in "The Golden Goose"—and film characters as well. Try to think of characters about whom you have mixed feelings. What about the not-very-talkative young man who volunteers in the same local garden that you do? Sometimes, you feel like he keeps quiet because he's standoffish and judgmental, but you've seen him be very tender with the flowers. Or what about the counterwoman at the local deli who's gruff, but cooks the most delicious egg-and-cheese sandwiches you've ever had? These may seem simpler than the hero of *Notes from Underground*, but that character was an ordinary person, too. There's no reason the counterwoman at the deli has to be any less complex than he was. It all depends on how you flesh out her characteristics.

Once you've come up with 10, choose one and spend a little time thinking about what gives you mixed feelings about this character. Very often, we smooth out our impressions of people, registering them in our minds as nicer than they are, or meaner than they are. Your mission here is to resist that impulse, to dig down to your real, mixed—complicated—feelings about this person. Draw two columns in your notebook, one labeled "Positive," the other "Negative." Find five qualities to place in each. Don't worry about whether your impressions are very nice or not, or very polite or not. Nobody will see this page—not even your mentor, if you don't want her to. If it makes you more comfortable, pretend that the character in question isn't real, and invent the negative characteristics.

Once your columns are filled, start writing your narrative description of the character, working around the qualities you mentioned in the columns. Build the profiles out as much as you can. So, for instance, your columns may look like this (using the example of the volunteer in the local garden):

Positive	Negative
1. Tender with flowers	1. Shy and standoffish
2. Knows a lot about flowers	2. Was mean to his mom when she came to pick him up
3. Spoke to another boy whom everyone ignores	3. Laughed at volunteer coordinator
4. Seems not to care whether anyone likes him	4. Seems not to care whether anyone likes him
5. Writes in a journal every day	5. Never joins the coordinator's team-building exercises

Note that it's hard to tell, with certain qualities, such as #4, whether they're positive or negative. So I included it in both columns.

Your narrative description may start like this:

Justin is a fellow volunteer at the local garden. He's as gruff as he's gentle. He's gentle with the flowers and gruff with everyone else. Well, that's not fully true. He's probably the only person at the garden who seems to like talking to Jason, who always has snot running down his shirt. We all flock to Sammy, the volunteer coordinator—I think the girls have a crush on him—but Justin seems to dislike Sammy. Sometimes, he'll laugh out loud at something Sammy is saying, though there's nothing particularly funny or ridiculous about it. Sammy's just trying to help us rebuild this public garden—the only one we have in our town. Sammy travels the country, helping communities build vegetable and flower gardens for public use. [And so on.]

Note several things:

1. As I was writing the portrait, it expanded to include a characterization of Sammy, the volunteer coordinator. Note that Sammy is complicated, too—our ally Justin doesn't seem to like him, but Sammy's mission is noble and he's just trying to do his job.

2. Note also the point of view that begins to emerge in the segment—the narrator seems to be a distant, quiet observer who notes (perhaps with some envy?) that the girls seem to like Sammy. Perhaps the narrator is male and a little jealous of Sammy. Perhaps the narrator is female and likes Justin even though the rest of the girls like Sammy. Either way, the narrator is emerging as a person slightly apart.

3. The portrait of Justin doesn't have to be built exclusively from actually observed characteristics of the real Justin at the real garden. Feel free to imagine what he's like at home, in other settings, walking his dog, talking back to his mom. When is he positive and when not so positive?

CHALLENGE EXERCISES

Notes 1 and 3, above, become challenge exercises:

1. Write 500-word narrative descriptions of two characters who are in conflict with each other but equally sympathetic.

2. Create a 500-word narrative portrait of a complicated character based on someone you know but filled mostly with imagined and invented details (i.e., Justin in settings other than where you've observed him).

DIALOGUE

LISTENING TO YOURSELF TALK

Purpose: To pay close attention to how spoken speech sounds.

I'm borrowing the concept for this exercise from a wonderful book called *What If? Writing Exercises for Fiction Writers* by Anne Bernays and Pamela Painter. If you enjoy it, check out the book.

You'll need an assistant—perhaps your mentor?—with whom you can disagree about something. One of you will represent one viewpoint and the other an opposing one. Then you'll need to disagree! What might your disagreement be about? The authors of *What If?* propose a shoplifting excursion where one of the two shoplifters gets cold feet. Another idea, closer to home, is that your mentor wants you to clean your room and you are very earnestly trying to persuade her that it's good for rooms to stay dirty. Or come up with your own idea.

You're going to record yourself disagreeing with the other person. If inventing a fictional disagreement is likely to make you self-conscious and too aware that you're acting, just record an ordinary conversation. The idea is to forget that you're being recorded. One way to make that happen is to ask a third person to be a secret recorder. That is, to hit "record" so the two "actors" don't know exactly when they're being taped. This way, the conversation is bound to be natural.

The conversation—and recording—should go on for at least three minutes. **When the recording is complete, transcribe the dialogue.**

How to transcribe: Skip the "uh"s and "eh"s, the way published dialogue mostly does, but you may wish to include **dialogue tags** or **descriptors** such as "Mom laughed," or "I yelled," or "Mom knocked on the table." By the same token, don't "clean" up the dialogue, inserting a word like "in" in a sentence like "Best thing you can do this situation." People swallow words. Dialogue should render that. It should also aim to render inflection—the way people change the pitch and tone of their voices as they talk. One thing you'll notice when you start paying close attention to dialogue is that people often say declarative things as if they're questions. Dialogue that looks like this: "That house we looked at today? I liked it." is better than dialogue that goes like this: "That house we looked at today—I liked it." A transcriber of human speech (a.k.a. a fiction writer) has to get really clever to render in print the many ways in which people inflect their speech. For instance, if someone is making a point of enunciating each word, as if annoyed—"What do you want?"—you could render it as "What. Do. You. Want?" or "What, do, you, want?" An alternative is to write:

> "What do you want?" he said, stabbing each word.

If the speaker drops his g's or otherwise somehow mispronounces letters or words, render that:

> "Stop cryin'!"

> "I'm tryin'!"

Of course, this can get comical and superfluous—it's a common way of speaking for everyone—so you may choose to ignore this particular departure from the standard. Same goes for the "d" most people drop when they say "and" or the way they pronounce "of" "aw." But if someone says "I brung it" instead of "I brought it" or "Looky here" instead of "Look here," your dialogue had better reflect it, no matter how grammatically incorrect it is. In short, to render dialogue, you have to get a little creative, in a Literary MacGyver kind of way. (If you don't know who MacGyver was, look him up online.)

When you've transcribed the dialogue, do one more thing. **Read through your dialogue and ask yourself: What about it is surprising, revealing, or different from the way it registered in your mind as you spoke it?** Typing out the spoken dialogue will serve as good practice in writing words between quotation marks that truly sound said, rather than written.

This exercise suggests a helpful trick for improving dialogue in a story: When you're done writing a story, read the dialogue out loud. Does it sound stilted or smooth? Straining to be casual or naturally casual? You might want to recruit others to act it out with you. How does it sound to them?

CHALLENGE EXERCISES

1. Eavesdropping with a tape recorder: *You* be the secret recorder. Record and transcribe a (nonprivate), several-minute-long conversation.

2. Build a fragment of plot around the disagreement dialogue (if you did that version of the exercise). You may have one already if you invented a reason for the two speakers to disagree. Tweak the dialogue so that it reads like part of a story about this subject rather than pure dialogue. That is, revise the dialogue where necessary, and—between the speaking lines—add new details from the author, such as the setting, who's wearing what, who's telling the story, etc. Also, provide information that tells us more about the characters. For instance:

Original recording (shoplifting exercise):

"Let's split, this was a bad idea."

"Life on the lam? Not for me."

Revised version:

"Let's split, why don't we?" Charlie rubbed his nose with his hand. How you knew the guy was nervous. He could rub his nose off when we were on the couch watching the last minutes of a football game. "This was a bad idea, Ruby."

I put my hands on his shoulders and looked him in the eyes. You just had to talk to him like a parent and he'd settle down. The fraternity brothers had been very clear: 'Come back with a pair of shoplifted white socks and you're in. Walk out of the store empty-handed and you're out.' They took our wallets and everything.

"Charlie," I said. "We are going to do this. You are going to do this. Let's go."

GOING FURTHER WITH DIALOGUE

Purpose: To refresh our understanding of how dialogue works in fiction.

Back to "The Golden Goose"! How would you describe the dialogue in "The Golden Goose"? Let's look at the very first line we encounter: "Do give me a piece of that cake you have got in your pocket, and let me have a draught of your wine—I am so hungry and thirsty." The first thing we notice is that this story must be from a pretty old time—no one says "draught" for "drink" nowadays. If you had a modern-day character say the same thing, it would probably sound something like: "Hey, I'm really hungry and thirsty. Can I have a piece of that cake and a drink from your bottle?" (Or, even more likely: "Hey, can I have a bite of your sandwich and a sip of your soda?")

Dialogue is tricky. As you discovered last week, most of us speak very differently from the way we write. We speak much less formally. It's as if, when we write, some inner schoolteacher comes out and harangues us to remember those commas. Certainly, most fiction is grammatical. But when it comes to dialogue, those rules have to go out the window. With dialogue the mission is to represent the way people really speak. And people—as you'll see once again in next week's exercise—don't speak with anything approaching grammatical formality.

Your mission this week is to rewrite the dialogue in "The Golden Goose" in the way people speak today. Reread "The Golden Goose" as it is printed in Appendix II. Pay special attention to the dialogue, which has been bolded. Then rewrite each line of dialogue as I have done with the opening line of dialogue above.

The first thing you have to do is figure out how much you are going to change your plot to suit your dialogue. In a great example of how interconnected the 5 Essentials are, you can hardly update the dialogue in the story without having to change some of its plot points. (Else, why are there old men granting wishes, and kings in the present day? Then again, that might make for a very unusual and interesting story.)

If your plot is going to stay largely the same, your new dialogue can preserve the details of the original, updating only the words. As above, "Do give me a piece of that cake you have got in your pocket, and let me have a draught of your wine—I am so hungry and thirsty" can become "Hey, I'm really hungry and thirsty. Can I have a piece of that cake and a drink from your bottle?" or "Hey, can I have a bite of your sandwich and a sip of your soda?" But if you choose to alter the plot so that only its basic premise remains—say, Dullhead is Dustin, and his great wish is to go to college, but his parents don't think he's up to it—the king could become a fraternity that won't admit him unless he meets certain challenges. Your dialogue will have to do more than simply come up with modern-day equivalents for words like "draught."

CHALLENGE EXERCISE

I bet the modernized dialogue you came up with suggested a modern plot, too, with the same basic outline as "The Golden Goose"—a dimwitted but kind individual, prevailing against odds to achieve a goal—but in a more modern setting. Re*plot* (in at least 10 plot points) "The Golden Goose" as a modern story.

DIALOGUE AS PLOT

Purpose: To tell a story using only dialogue.

This week, you're going to write a 500-word segment in which two people talk to each other. The catch is that this segment will feature nothing other than dialogue, except **dialogue tags** such as "he said" or "she said" or "the sheriff said" so that we can distinguish who's speaking.

In other words, the dialogue itself will have to tell us readers everything we need to know. This is known as folding the plot into the dialogue. Of course, it would be silly if the characters did this too obviously: "As you know, Winston, the door has been broken for over a year." If Winston and Winona are husband and wife, then Winston would know very well that the door is broken. He would hardly need Winona to tell him. So, the characters *need to have a reason to be telling each other what they're telling each other.* For instance, if you need your readers to know that, say, the crop was a bust last year, you could have Winona say something like: "You bought them fancy tractors, and so what—the crop was still a bust last year, save for the blueberries." Officially, Winona sounds like she's haranguing Winston for his fancy-tractor habit. But while she is, the author sneaks in the information that the crop was a bust last year. It's part of her harangue, and it doesn't sound as forced and obvious this way.

AN ASIDE ABOUT DETAIL:

By the way, Winona's mention of "blueberries" makes the line sound even more "real." Why so? Because its what's called an "authenticating detail." You'll learn more about these in the next level, but for now, let me explain the concept with the help of Gabriel

García Márquez, a Nobel Prize-winning Colombian novelist who is most famous for his novel *One Hundred Years of Solitude*. As he told the literary journal *The Paris Review* in 1981, "if you say there are elephants flying in the sky, people are not going to believe you. But if you say there are four hundred and twenty-five elephants flying in the sky, people will probably believe you." Why? Because the specificity of that "four hundred and twenty-five" makes it sound like it really happened. It's as if the reader thinks: "This person couldn't be making it up if it's so specific." When people are making stuff up—whether in life or in fiction—the dead giveaway is: Things are too general. It's hard to invent with as much detail as real life presents us. The best authors do.

Back to our assignment. Another thing you'll have to fold into the dialogue is a sense, for the reader, of what the characters are feeling toward each other. When you're not under the restrictions of an assignment like this one, you can write things like "the sheriff said sourly" or "the sheriff said jauntily." You can also indicate the character's disposition by having him do something that *shows* he's sour or jaunty—for instance, "the sheriff said, driving his knuckles into the metal filing cabinet." (Notice the authenticating detail in that sentence—"*metal filing* cabinet," not just "cabinet.") So, how might you make the sheriff's mood clear in the dialogue? Instead of saying something like "Hands together" to a prisoner, you could have him say, "Hands together, filth" if you want him to be angry; "Hands together, now," if you want him to sound a little tentative; "Hands together, Mr. McCree. I got to do this," if you want to indicate that the sheriff's got a relationship with the prisoner.

Here's some sample dialogue that tries to fold in plot, character descriptions and relationships—that is, tell the reader everything the reader needs to know about what's going on.

"Think we can make it?" the first boy said.

"From here to the woods? That's a hundred yards, at least. They'll see us. Brilliant idea to break into the Clews castle, just brilliant."

"I thought it was empty!"

"You thought! Well, at least you thought. Sometimes, you forget to do that."

"Hey, I had a gun to your head? You could've stayed home."

"In this town? Even the jail is better than staying at home."

"Can you hear those dogs?" the first boy said.

"No. That ain't dogs, is it? Tell me that's not dogs."

"Why they got dogs snooping around? Wait a minute. Maybe there's something in that castle. Of course there is. Why would they have an alarm like that on a castle with nothing in it?"

"Because, you know, it's somebody's home, and some people, strange as it seems, aren't too fond of having their homes broken into."

"I'm making a run for it."

"Excuse me, what about me?" the second boy said.

~

So, what's the plot here? Two boys have broken into a castle, which tripped the alarm and brought out a frightening show of law enforcement, as if the castle contains something really secretive.

How did I convey this? Look at Line 2. The second boy rags on the first boy for his "brilliant idea" of breaking into the castle. As readers, we're focused on his ragging, on grasping that this second boy probably criticizes the first one quite frequently—a character trait, and a clue about their relationship. But as we're focused on that, the author slips in a plot factoid. Note the authenticating specific detail, by the way—not just the castle: the "*Clews* castle."

Characters: We've got the first boy and the second boy. We don't even know their names. But we do know quite a bit about their personalities and relationship. As I already discussed, line 2, where the second boy sarcastically chews out the first, shows us that he probably looks down on his friend. The first boy's initial response is to defend himself, as if he wants to persuade his friend to raise his opinion of him. Only then does he get his back up and remind his friend that he didn't have to come. At first the second boy pretends he came only because he was bored—a comment through which we learn that this is probably a small town with so little to do. When the first boy hears dogs, he starts to piece things together—the dogs, the alarm—that the second boy, for all his supposed intelligence, hasn't, and so we're getting the idea that for all the high-handedness of the second boy, it's the first boy who's got the smarts to get them out of this situation. The second boy continues sarcastically lighting into the first one—some people put alarms in their homes because they don't want them broken into—but when the first boy says he's making a run for it, the second boy shows some of his true colors. The prissy, fearful way in which he makes the exchange's last comment makes us realize that when push comes to shove, he's going to be hiding behind his friend.

As you can see, you can fold a LOT of information into dialogue. How might you do it in your assignment?

For starters, come up with a situation, a reason for two people to be talking. You don't have to flesh this situation out too much. Look out your window, and if you see two pigeons sitting on a wire, you can have them talk to each other. As for what exactly their concerns are in the dialogue—in other words, what your plot is—you can go back to the early lessons of this fiction section for guidance. You could map out what they're discussing in advance or find it along the way, starting yourself off with nothing more than a first sentence; if you do map out in advance, you can map out with a lot of detail or a little.

You'll want to know some basics about your characters. Do they like each other? Hate each other? What do they want? (Remember, that's the most important question about a character, along with "Who is he/she?") In the case of my two boys, I would have answered that they have a somewhat barbed relationship, as many boys do. In a basic sense, they both want to get out of the situation they're in, but they have other wants, too: The first boy probably resents the second for cutting into him all the time; the second probably resents the first for being braver and more resourceful and so tries to put him down.

Of course, you can also write dialogue that doesn't have so much folded in:

"How are you?"

"Well."

"What are you doing today?"

"Flying around a bit. Looking for crumbs. The usual."

~

There's no situation that needs resolution here—our pigeons are just discussing their day, like a mom and dad about to go off to work—and the wants of the characters aren't the kind to pull a reader in. But this kind of dialogue may be a helpful stepping stone to something more complex. If you feel overwhelmed by folding all sorts of information into your dialogue, just start writing down a conversation between two people. You can always go back and work on changing a few words to convey a better sense of character and situation.

Whichever you do, remember: 500 words.

CHALLENGE EXERCISES

1. Write 10 individual sentences, each of which features an authenticating detail; that is, something specific that makes the reader think, "Oh, that must have really happened." Example: "I unloaded the bales from the bed of the pickup, still scratched up from the rebar last week." An author less obsessed with the authenticating detail might write, "I unloaded the bales from the bed of the pickup." That's fine. But that sounds like one generic pickup. The specific detail that follows brings it alive, makes it sound like not *a* pickup, but *the* pickup—the specific pickup in this specific story.

2. Rewrite your dialogue assignment from the lesson, adding as much outside-of-dialogue text as you'd like: clarifying adverbs after dialogue tags, actions by the characters, explanation from the author about what's what. Since you're

importing that information into the text of the story itself, you'll want to lose it from the dialogue. Do you see how much simpler the dialogue becomes as a result? Forcing dialogue under the pressure of having to say everything makes it wonderfully rich, richer than when you have help from other devices. Something to keep in mind. Dialogue has to do several things at the same time—provide information, tell a story, convey personality, and so forth—or it sounds too simple. Gabbing away about nothing with your friends is perfectly natural in the "real world." But on a page it seems too casual. Think of the written page as some very expensive real estate. You can't use up too much land as you build on it, and you have to find room for all your appliances and cars and backyard garden in one little patch.

SETTING

SETTING

**Purpose: To learn more about how setting works
by updating the setting of "The Golden Goose."**

Usually, the setting is the background to the events of the story, but don't mistake "background" for "insignificant." Setting is critical. When an author forgets to situate the story in *some* place—it could be real or not, but it has to be reasonably well fleshed out—the story kind of floats, even if the author has taken care of his plot, characters, dialogue, and point of view with skill. Just think about how important setting is in "The Golden Goose." Think about how much the early scenes in the forest create the atmosphere of enchantment that we associate with fairy tales. The "inn" hints to us that this is a rural place rather than a big city, and "inn," you'll agree, suggests an older time than "hotel." The same goes for the parson, the clerk, and the peasants. The presence of these characters suggests again that we're in a rural place, and, again, probably some time ago—we'd call "peasants" "farmers" nowadays, probably.

What you're seeing in "The Golden Goose" is a presentation of setting, so to speak, between the lines. The story doesn't take any time out to describe the setting of the story directly, such as: "Dullhead lived with two brothers and their parents in a small country in the middle of Europe. It rained a lot, so the fields were always lush with green plants, and the trees grew mighty and tall. Because it was so damp, it was chilly most of the year, so each home had a large fireplace for those bone-cold autumn and winter nights. The dry season only lasted three months, so the months of June, July, and August were filled with families traipsing to the woods to cut down trees for winter heating."

This direct approach isn't necessarily better or worse, just different from the between-the-lines approach of the fairy tale as it is. My example above aims to complement the tale's atmosphere of enchantment, because rain is, well, atmospheric. Secondly, it suggests a climate of natural abundance. What does that have to do with our story? Maybe nothing directly. But imagine if this tale took place in a desert, where little grows and the sun beats down mercilessly? For me, that kind of story brings up thoughts of privation and a fight for survival, whereas a story that takes place in a rich natural climate makes me imagine fertility, abundance, and the possibility of growth and developments. Put more simply, in a desert, things die. In a lush field, they thrive. If you had to pick a setting for a story about a golden goose and a marriage between an ordinary young man and a king's daughter, which setting would you pick? You could pick either, but they would be two very different stories.

What the above paragraphs get into is how much setting suggests a story's **atmosphere**. If our story takes place on a farm where everything is in a state of disrepair—the shingles on the roof of the barn are missing, the horses are lean—it won't surprise us to learn that this is a home of grief. (Perhaps someone has died, or the area has been suffering through hard times.) Conversely, imagine what you might feel if a story takes place in a culinary school, amid gleaming industrial kitchens with the latest equipment and sharp knives. You're probably going to feel energy, intensity, an adrenaline rush—it won't surprise you to learn that the school has a cutthroat competition for a chance to cook for a week at a major restaurant in New York—but it will definitely feel different from what you felt in the previous setting, right?

Settings can be intended to be real or obviously invented. If we're on planet Xeron, or if we're in an enchanted wood with a golden goose, we realize that we're clearly in invented territory. But this doesn't mean that the authors of such fiction can do whatever they please. Think about how you'd feel as a reader if a spaceship crashed the proceedings in "The Golden Goose"? You'd say to yourself: No way! This is because even in an obviously nonrealistic setting, the setting has to have an internal logic; which is to say: You better have a darn good reason for having a spaceship invade a story that takes place long before spaceships existed. Now, if you're writing a story that's meant to be outlandish and kooky, maybe it's okay. But, as I've already mentioned several times, it's important to understand the effect your decisions will have on your audience.

If your intention is to create a fictional world that's meant to feel exactly like its real counterpart—that is, if your plan is to tell a realistic story—you'll have to work really hard and provide a lot of specific, concrete details. It'll probably be hard to persuade readers that a story is taking place in a "real" mill town in Kansas without an understanding of how mills work (and, more important, what it might be like to live in a mill town).

To be clear, it's perfectly possible to write a story in which the setting doesn't have a large role. You could mention that the story takes place in a mill town and then never refer to it again because your concern is a mysterious set of events that has less to do with *where* this takes place than what exactly goes down. (And it's something that would be mysterious *anywhere*).

What I want you to realize is that setting can deeply influence how a story reads to an audience. This isn't a formal assignment, but next time you read a short story or longer fiction, try to pay attention to setting. (While remembering that setting comes in many guises—not only in physical descriptions of the place, but in between-the-lines hints such as we get in "The Golden Goose.") As you're reading, grab your notebook and jot down the feelings inspired by the setting. As readers, we often take these details for granted. As budding authors, we have to start being mechanics. We have to lift the hood of a story and try to figure out how it was put together, so we can do something like it ourselves when our turn comes. We have to start thinking like authors.

To that end, your exercise this week will be to do for setting in "The Golden Goose" what you did for dialogue several weeks ago: Update it. This will be a handy way of isolating all the moments—some direct, some not—where setting comes into play in the story. The big challenge here is *consistency*. As I hope you've gathered, where exactly you set a story is less important than making sure to be consistent with its details, or you risk having your reader throw up his hands and shout, "This is made up!" (Well, *of course* it is, but the fiction writer's great sleight of hand is to make the reader forget that.) If your story takes place in a medieval village, a Ford pickup truck probably shouldn't appear. If it rains every month except June, July, and August, you probably shouldn't have a sunny day in November. If it's a poor mill town, everyone in town shouldn't be rich, etc.

So, your assignment: Rewrite "The Golden Goose," updating it to modern times. (I provide an example below.) You may wish to spend a little time preparing in advance. Choose several paragraphs, underline those details that relate to setting, figure out how to preserve the general theme of the story (a disadvantaged sibling, his act of kindness, a reward, a set of challenges by a powerful figure with a gift to bestow...) while shifting the setting to modern times. You may have some ideas already, from preparing for your update of the tale's dialogue several weeks ago. Don't worry too much about picking a setting that will accommodate all the fairy tale's themes. Its themes are universal, and most settings, from a college to a factory to a car race, will give you an opportunity to invoke them.

If you want a little inspiration, you can compare a recent film with the classic book on which it's based. For instance, the 1995 film *Clueless* is an update of the Jane Austen novel *Emma*. Emma is Emma Woodhouse, a well-to-do young woman in 19th century England obsessed with playing matchmaker for various people in her social circle. Cher Horowitz, in *Clueless*, is a well-to-do young woman in 1990s Beverly Hills who loves playing matchmaker for various people in her circle, too. And she, too, learns something about love and what's important in life but in very different circumstances than her model.

Here's my stab at reinventing the setting of "The Golden Goose," starting at the beginning. If you'd like, you can use it as a departure point for your own retelling of setting. Or you can also retell the beginning paragraphs, as I did, only don't copy the way I updated the story! You'll see that prior to starting I made a decision about where I was going to update this story. (I decided to continue with my college idea from the dialogue update in Week 9.)

"The Golden Goose," Reimagined

THERE was once a man who had three sons. The youngest of them was called Dullhead, and was sneered and jeered at and snubbed on every possible opportunity.

One day it happened that the eldest son wished to go **to college**, and before he started his mother **bought him lots of clothes and schoolbooks**, so that he might be sure not to suffer from **his classmates' ridicule**.

When he reached the **college** he met a little old grey man **by the large iron gates** who wished him "Good morning," and said: "Do give me **one of your shirts and maybe a book to read?** My shirt is all rags and I could use a new book. I didn't have the money to go to college, but I still like to learn."

But this clever son replied: "If I give you my **clothes and books** I shall have none left for myself; you just go your own way;" and he left the little man standing there and went further on **into the dry, gray fields that covered the school grounds**. There he began to **take classes and play sports**, but before long he **hurt himself in the pole vault, and smacked his head** so badly that he was obliged to go home and **take a semester off, delaying his degree and putting his scholarship in danger**.

$\sim$

See what I did? Once I decided to rewrite the story on a college campus, the other details fell into place much more easily. One other note: Did you notice that I made the fields covering the school "dry" and "gray"? I didn't have to do that. I could have simply said "fields." But I wanted to indicate to the reader, between the lines, that this place of schooling might be intellectually impressive, but is missing something critical, like kindness and heart, as symbolized by this new student the college has accepted. You'll remember us discussing lush fields as a symbol of fertility and the possibility of birth or good developments, and desert as a symbol of the opposite. That's the symbolism I was tapping into with my description of the fields as "dry" and "gray." We'll talk about **symbolism** more in the future. It can be simplistic (desert = death, field = life), but it can also be quite nuanced, and if we know the difference, we can help our stories be much richer.

Now, your turn!

CHALLENGE EXERCISE

1a. Make a list of 15 verbs, nouns, adjectives, and adverbs that the setting of "The Golden Goose" (the real version) makes you think of or feel. For me, as you may have gleaned up above, the list would include words like forest, woods, enchanting, atmosphere, rain, fields, green, etc. Note that some of these words appear in the story but others do not. The goal here is to try to put into language the feelings provoked by the setting, whether directly or between the lines.

1b. When you're finished, reread a favorite short story that's set in a very different kind of place. Do the same for that story.

USING SETTING TO CREATE A MOOD IN A SHORT STORY

Purpose: To learn how to use setting to create atmosphere in fiction.

As we discussed last week, where a story takes place has a lot to do with how we read the story. Think about it: If the first paragraph of a story tells us that the story is taking place in a beat-up old barn in a county that's been experiencing drought, we feel one thing. If it tells us that we're in the middle of the ocean during a squall, we feel something else. If we're in an airplane, we feel yet a third thing, and so on.

Just read this paragraph from the novel *Sentimental Education* by the great 19th-century French novelist Gustave Flaubert:

> Then he slowly toiled up the streets again. The gas lamps vibrated, casting on the mud long yellowish shafts of flickering light. Shadowy forms surmounted by umbrellas glided along the footpaths. The pavement was slippery; the fog grew thicker, and it seemed to him that the moist gloom, wrapping him around, descended into the depths of his heart.[3]

---

3 Flaubert, Gustave. *Sentimental Education*, in *The Complete Works of Gustave Flaubert, Vol. 5–6*, trans. Anonymous. (Minneapolis, MN: CyberPoet Press, 2011), Kindle edition.

Before you go on, tell me quickly what the above paragraph made you imagine or feel. Just say or write down the first three words that come to your mind.

What did you come up with? Sad, downcast, gloomy, depressing? That effect is created by nothing more than a description of a place. Nowhere but in the last line of the paragraph does the author actually spell out for us how our hero is feeling.

Your job this week will be to fill two pages in your notebook with four entries (approximately 250 words each, for a total of 1000 words) directly describing places that will elicit the assigned emotions below. Do you remember what I meant by describing a place directly? ("Dullhead lived with two brothers and their parents in a small country in the middle of Europe. It rained a lot, so the fields were always lush with green plants, and the trees grew mighty and tall ...") See below for another example of what I mean.

In the future, you may want to use each entry as the first paragraph of a new story.

1. Depression; a sense of a place being down on its luck
2. Terror
3. Anxiety and uncertainty
4. Triumph, success, confidence

If you noticed, the first three correspond to the three examples I gave you in the first paragraph of this week's lesson (beat-up barn, ocean during a squall, on an airplane). Use them as examples if you're stumped, or come up with your own. With the fourth, you'll have to come up with the whole thing from scratch.

A direct description of the beat-up old barn could begin: "The barn was all alone in a field as flat as a cutting board. Pop hadn't had the money to repaint since 2004, so you were liable to get a piece of plaster on your head if you weren't too careful. We grew alfalfa, soybeans, and corn. Never enough for more than two meals a day. We all slept in the barn.

It had soaring ceilings, sparrows flitting among the rafters. (Once in a while, you got a present on your head from them, too.)"

Note, in the above example, the way other plot details crept into my description of setting, suggesting ideas for a story. In fact, I ended up with a less-than-direct description of the barn. (A strictly direct one would start: "The barn was as red as a firehouse. It had soaring ceilings, but that was it for grand details. The paint was peeling, and some corners you didn't walk into because you'd get tangled up in cobwebs thicker than a fishing net.") If that's what happens to you, too, that's fine.

CHALLENGE EXERCISES

1a. Describe a place without worrying about what kind of feeling it conjures. Refer back to your lessons on description to brush up on description skills. Write 500 words. The segment could be about your kitchen, your yard, or some place in town. (Ask your mentor to drive you there and let you spend some time observing it and taking notes.) After you've finished, answer this question: Does the description you ended up with conjure any particular feeling?

1b. Describe that feeling using three adjectives.

1c. Then ask your mentor to read the segment and describe the feeling conjured by it in three adjectives. (Without having seen your adjectives.)

POINT OF VIEW

BASIC POINT OF VIEW

Purpose: To understand the differences between first- and third-person points of view.

Compare these two sentences:

1. Josh grabbed the wheelbarrow.
2. I grabbed the wheelbarrow.

In the first sentence, someone who isn't Josh is providing the information. Who is it? We don't know. It could be someone who is also a character in the story, or it could be someone who's "offstage," so to speak—that is, not a part of the story. We refer to this someone as a **third-person narrator.**

In the second sentence, the story is being told by an "I," or a first-person narrator.

Is the narrator of "The Golden Goose" first or third person?

If you answered third, you're correct. A critical difference between first-person and third-person narrators is that a first-person narrator tends to know only what's going on his own mind. A third-person narrator, if he's all-knowing—and that's the kind we'll focus on for now—tends to know what's going in everyone's minds. Think of him or her as a superhero who can fly into anyone's thoughts.

A first-person narrator is also, by definition, a part of the story. A third-person narrator doesn't have to be, but could be. So, to recap the major differences:

THE DIFFERENCE BETWEEN FIRST-PERSON
AND THIRD-PERSON NARRATORS

First Person	Third Person
"I"	"he," "she," "they"
All-knowing? No. Knows only what's going on his or her own mind.	**All-knowing?** More so than first person.
Part of the story? Yes.	**Part of the story?** Not necessarily, but possibly.

Is the narrator of "The Golden Goose" all-knowing? Seems to be; he not only describes the events of the story, but contextualizes them by explaining to us the inner motivations of the characters. (The parents don't think much of Dullhead; the king is reluctant to give his daughter away to him; etc.) Is the narrator part of the story? No. Do we know who he or she or it is? We don't.

This week, your exercise will be to rewrite a section of "The Golden Goose" from the first-person point of view of one of the characters: the goose, the king, Dullhead's father, or anyone else in the story.

Below are a couple of lines from a sample retelling from the perspective of the goose. The goose is a good narrator to choose because he's present for the entire story; if you choose the king, you'd have to get pretty inventive to figure out how the king could know about the early events of the story (the chopping in the forest by the brothers) or even the later ones (presumably the king doesn't know how Dullhead finds the solutions to his challenges). Since your assignment is to do only a section—exactly how much is defined below—you may not have this problem, but having to invent a way for the king to know about the early events of the story (maybe he has spies everywhere in the land?) presents intriguing plot challenges.

Whatever character you choose as your narrator, try really hard to put yourself in her shoes. Think about what she knows and doesn't know. Think about how she might see things, considering her motives and interests. What does she want in the world of the story? In what way is she inclined to spin the story? What kind of mood is she in? Remember: Each narrator has her own perspective, motives, etc.

Sample Retelling
From the Perspective of the Goose

Can you imagine what it's like to sit inside a tree for one thousand years? I didn't think so. I'll have you know as well that my feathers are made of gold. And gold, my friends, weighs a lot more than ordinary down feathers, which you people just love to pluck from the bodies of my fellow geese and stuff into your pillows. Well, you can say that I was created as a kind of revenge; just you try to pluck a feather off me.

In any case, like I said, I'd been sitting in this tree, on assignment from He Who Is The Most Powerful, for a thousand years. It was a nice tree, all in all, if you have to sit somewhere for a thousand years: an old oak, a little damp inside but manageable, with all sorts of dainty critters running around. I require no food for survival, you see, but once in a while, it gets mighty lonesome deep inside a big oak, and it sure is fun to have some company, even if your company is a bunch of maggots.

But, really, I should get on with my story. He Who Is The Most Powerful made it clear: You will get to emerge from the tree when someone in the country has done a kindness to the Little Old Grey Man who wanders around the woods. Well, that must be one unkind country because it took a thousand years for me to finally emerge. Here's how it happened.

I hope you'll note a couple of things about the above retelling. It preserves some things from the original story, like the fact that the goose has feathers made of gold. But it also invents some things out of nowhere, such as the fact that the tree is an oak, that the goose has been waiting for a thousand years and is there on assignment from He Who Is The Most Powerful, whoever that is.

I also decided that the goose would have a pretty conversational speaking style. Notice all the examples of that ("In any case," "like I said"). By the way, I didn't so much "decide" this as sort of "listen" to the goose, as we've discussed in lessons on character and dialogue. I didn't plan; rather, I started writing, and found myself speaking as the goose in a pretty light-hearted, conversational, and even somewhat taunting voice.

Finally, note one last thing: This particular retelling breaks down the "wall" between the storyteller and his audience. In the original story, there is no acknowledgment by the narrator, whoever that is, that he is telling a story. In this version, the goose mentions the story directly: "But, really, I should get on with my story." This isn't a big deal but these different ways of telling a story each create a different effect on the reader. A narrator who doesn't acknowledge telling a story feels remote, distant, perhaps trustworthy on account of his distance and remoteness, but also not very easy to imagine as a friend or ally. The goose, on the other hand, is obviously much more personable, if not necessarily trustworthy. (If you've ever been the target of a salesman's pitch, you know that friendliness doesn't have to equal trustworthiness.)

To paraphrase the goose: "But, really, let's get on with our exercise for this week!" It's your turn to retell a section of "The Golden Goose" from a different perspective. If you'd like a real challenge, retell the whole story. But you're likely to get a good idea of the challenges involved simply by retelling 500 words.

CHALLENGE EXERCISES

1. For your three favorite short stories (or three random ones if you don't have favorites), answer these questions:

   a. Is the narrator first- or third-person?
   b. Is the narrator part of the story?
   c. If the narrator is third-person, does he seem to know what everyone is thinking all the time?

2. "The Golden Goose" has an all-knowing third-person narrator. In your main exercise this week, you retold a part of the story from the perspective of a first-person narrator. Now retell the story using a narrator who is not all-knowing, be it third- or first-person. (Refer back to the explanation at the start of this lesson for a refresher.) The king would actually be a great narrator to choose here, because he has no access to the early events of the story so he doesn't know who Dullhead is, where he comes from, or why he has this entourage trailing him. Rewrite a section of the story—the last third would seem to be the natural section to rewrite—from the perspective of the king, as he tries to understand who all these people are and where they come from.

FIRST-PERSON VS. THIRD-PERSON NARRATION

**Purpose: To get a closer understanding of how
a story changes depending on who tells it.**

Last week, you retold "The Golden Goose"—which is told in third person—from the first-person point of view of another character in the story.

Moving on to this week's exercise, **your mission is to write a 250-word scene twice (for a total of around 500 words). First, write the scene in the first person. Then rewrite it in third person.** You'll see how many ways the telling shifts when you move from first to third.

The scene can take any form you like: You could give us the inner thoughts of a character. You can include dialogue or action, too. (Examples of both are below.) In your third-person narration, you can have a character who is part of the story or some off-stage narrator who never identifies himself. Also, this third-person narrator can be very knowledgeable about the thoughts, feelings, and motivations of other characters. Or he can be limited only by what he knows.

So, this exercise asks you to do three things:

1. Practice first- vs. third-person narration.
2. Try to understand the ways in which switching between first and third changes the kind of information that can appear in the story.
3. Try to acquaint yourself with the idea of an all-knowing narrator vs. one with limited knowledge.

Here's an example.

1. We watched the sun set from the rocks by the pier. I wanted to ask Qadir what the sunset was like in his hometown in Iraq. It has always been strange to me that you can travel thousands of miles and the sunset looks exactly the same. Well, maybe not exactly—I read somewhere that smog and pollution make sunsets more beautiful. They didn't have as much smog and pollution in Iraq as we did in San Diego, did they? That was another thing I wanted to ask Qadir. Also whether he missed home. Hurry up and learn English, I wanted to tell him. I have so many things I want to ask you.

2. Gene and Qadir watched the sun set from the rocks by the pier. The American boy swelled with pride as the water lapped the pylons because he was introducing the Iraqi boy, a refugee, to a new vision. Gene's father had  served in the First Iraq War, and the few things he had said about it to his son made the boy think of the country as an endless desert. But in fact Qadir was from Basra, which was much closer to the Persian Gulf than the Minnesota from which Gene's parents had moved only a year before, because his father was reassigned to a military base in Southern California. Qadir had spent most of his life in fishing boats; he was taken from the hospital directly to the gulf, the joke in his family went. That's what Qadir thought of now, staring at the falling light beginning to silver the water: fishing by moonlight in the Gulf.

ANALYSIS

In the first example, we have a first-person "I" narrator—Gene. Gene tells the story from his own perspective. He's a player in the events. Gene knows only what's going on in his own mind, and not only because Qadir doesn't speak English.

In the second example, an all-knowing third-person narrator is giving us a peek into both boys' minds. We don't know who this narrator is—maybe he enters the story later, maybe not—but he does seem to know what's going on in everyone's minds.

A WORD ABOUT HOW TO CHOOSE PERSPECTIVE FOR YOUR STORY

If you're trying to decide whether to tell a story from the perspective of an "I" or a third-person narrator, remember that they have different advantages. A story told from a first-person point of view is likely to be more vivid and immediate—you're getting a broadcast from inside someone's mind, with all the intimacy that implies. A third-person narrator tends to be more removed, more sober, less conversational. But a third-person narrator's advantage is that he (or she, or it) can look inside people's minds in a way that tends to be much harder for a first-person narrator. Think of a first-person narrator as yourself in a way—do you know what everyone's thinking? No. For that you need a fictional superhero: the All-Knowing Third Person.

MORE ON THIRD-PERSON NARRATION

A third-person narration doesn't explicitly have to come from the inner thoughts of some third-person narrator, be he offstage or not. This, too, is third-person narration:

> Gene and Qadir walked toward the pier, the silence loud in Gene's ears. Gene searched his mind for something to say. Qadir only squinted at the shimmering water, as if he was trying to make out the end of the ocean, and beyond it, the country where he was born.
>
> "Can you swim?" Gene said, swimming through the air with his arms and pointing at the water.

"Yes," Qadir said in his hesitant English. "Very much."

～

This third-person narration includes dialogue and action as well. The narrator still seems to be all-knowing—"the silence loud in Gene's ears"—by the way.

DIFFERENCES BETWEEN FIRST PERSON AND THIRD PERSON IN WHAT A STORY CAN REVEAL

Let's go back to our original example. Were you able to notice the different kinds of information that a story is likely to present depending on whether it's told in first person or third?

There's the obvious difference of the #2 narrator knowing what's going on in Qadir's head, while #1 doesn't. In the first narrative, we learn more about how Gene sees things, which leaves open the question of how well he understands what Qadir is thinking. In #2, we learn about what's going in both boys' minds.

Also:

- Since Gene doesn't know what's in Qadir's mind and can't ask him because he doesn't speak English, he can only wonder what the sunsets are like in Iraq, which in turn makes him think of something he'd read about sunsets and smog, or how strange it is that you see the sun wherever you are in the world. None of this appears in #2, though it could.

- Narrator #2's knowledge—knowledge Gene doesn't possess in #1—that Qadir grew up near water occasions all sorts of information and detail. There's no way Gene can know that, because Qadir doesn't speak English. (Though, perhaps, later in the story, Qadir tries to explain this via gestures.)

- This knowledge makes it relevant for Narrator #2 to mention that Gene thinks of Iraq as a desert, thanks to what he was told by his father after serving in the First Iraq War; and that, in fact, they are more recent arrivals to coast living than Qadir. None of this occurs to Gene to mention in #1.

- And so on. You must know that neither approach is superior to the other. I just wanted you to notice how differently the narrative proceeds depending on who's doing the telling.

Now, it's your turn. Render the same moment for 250 words in first-person narration and then third-person narration. You should have at least two characters in your situation, or it won't make much sense. (Though you can have as many as you'd like.) For the first segment, pick a character through whose eyes you're going to observe (and interpret) the scene. For the second, become an all-knowing narrator who can see inside everyone's minds (and therefore correct the first person's errors of observation, if such exist). The first-person narrator doesn't have to be wrong about stuff, the way Gene is, above. He may simply be having one set of thoughts while another character has another, though that latter information is available only to a third-person narrator.

If you're stuck, here are some ideas for situations and characters:

- Monica and Vance are at a hockey game, because Vance is a rabid fan of the local team. Monica reluctantly agreed to come along. (She hates sports, but tries not to rub it in Vance's face.) Give us Monica—or Vance's—thoughts, and those of an all-seeing narrator.

- A bus is full of riders early one morning. Give us the thoughts of one, and a narrator who can get inside everyone's minds.

- A group of friends goes swimming in a lake. Get inside the mind of one in a first-person narration and then give us a bird's eye view by an all-knowing third-person narrator. What exactly is going in on this situation is up to you.

CHALLENGE EXERCISE

Write a 250-word segment from the first-person perspective of another character in the situation, such as Qadir in the situation in the lesson. (We get to hear only from Gene and the third-person narrator.)

STORY UNIT: THE SCENE

WRITING A SCENE FROM SCRATCH

Purpose: To incorporate all 5 Essentials in a single tableau.

You've practiced the 5 Essentials: Plot, Character, Dialogue, Setting, Point of View.

This week's assignment takes things to the next level because it asks you to think about all five at once. **You're going to invent a scene** that makes clear the plot of the story behind it; characters who are well-fleshed out despite appearing briefly; dialogue that feels convincing and lifelike; a setting that's palpable despite your having such a short space in which to convey it; and a point of view that reflects conscious choices by the author. (That's you!) That is a lot to achieve in a single scene of 500 words. Let's get organized by creating a checklist.

Your scene has to:

1. ☐ Make clear the plot of the story behind it.
2. ☐ Include characters who are well-fleshed out.
3. ☐ Feature dialogue that feels convincing and lifelike.
4. ☐ Present a palpable setting, whether directly or between the lines.
5. ☐ Be told from a concrete and consciously chosen point of view.

How to achieve this? Let's begin by considering a scene from a published story. Note the following: This scene takes place in a concrete place, involves action, and is finite in duration. The notes in capital letters and brackets throughout are from me. Words that may be unfamiliar to you are bolded. Look them up in the dictionary and record their definitions in your notebook. I bold words like "eminence" and "space" because, in this story, they are used differently from their traditional definitions.

From "The Valley of Spiders"

H. G. Wells

(opening 475 words)

Towards mid-day the three pursuers [CHARACTERS] came abruptly round a bend in the **torrent bed** upon the sight of a very broad and spacious valley. [SETTING] The difficult and winding trench of pebbles along which they had tracked the fugitives [PLOT] for so long expanded to a broad slope, and with a common impulse the three men left the trail and rode to a little **eminence** set with olive-dun trees [MORE DETAIL ON SETTING], and there halted, the two others, as became them, a little behind the man with the silver-studded **bridle**. [MORE DETAIL ON CHARACTERS]

For a **space** they scanned the great expanse below them with eager eyes. It spread remoter and remoter, with only a few clusters of **sere** thorn bushes here and there, and the dim suggestions of some now waterless ravine, to break its desolation of yellow grass. Its purple distances melted at last into the bluish slopes of the further hills—hills it might be of a greener kind— and above them invisibly supported, and seeming indeed to hang in the blue, were the snowclad summits of mountains that grew larger and bolder to the north-westward as the sides of the valley drew together. And west- ward the valley opened until a distant darkness under the sky told where the forests began. [MORE DETAIL ON SETTING] But the three men looked neither east nor west, but only steadfastly across the valley. [BACK TO PLOT]

The gaunt man with the scarred lip [PHYSICAL DESCRIPTION OF CHARAC- TER] was the first to speak. "Nowhere," he said, with a sigh of disappoint- ment in his voice. "But after all, they had a full day's start." [DIALOGUE; PLOT DETAIL]

"They don't know we are after them," said the little man on the white horse. [MORE PLOT VIA DIALOGUE]

"She would know," said the leader bitterly, as if speaking to himself. [PLOT MYSTERY; WE DON'T KNOW WHO OR WHAT HE MEANS]

"Even then they can't go fast. They've got no beast but the mule, and all to- day the girl's foot has been bleeding—" [MORE PLOT THROUGH DIALOGUE]

The man with the silver bridle flashed a quick intensity of rage on him. "Do you think I haven't seen that?" he snarled.

"It helps, anyhow," whispered the little man to himself.

The gaunt man with the scarred lip stared impassively. "They can't be over the valley," he said. "If we ride hard—"

He glanced at the white horse and paused.

"Curse all white horses!" said the man with the silver bridle, and turned to scan the beast his curse included.

The little man looked down between the melancholy ears of his steed.

"I did my best," he said. [MORE PLOT MYSTERY; WE DON'T KNOW QUITE WHAT HE'S REFERRING TO]

The two others stared again across the valley for a space. The gaunt man passed the back of his hand across the scarred lip.

"Come up!" said the man who owned the silver bridle, suddenly. The little man started and jerked his rein, and the horse hoofs of the three made a **multitudinous** faint pattering upon the withered grass as they turned back towards the trail. …

～

    Plot: We don't know the plot in detail, but we know enough to want to keep reading. These characters are tracking someone they refer to as "fugitives." (That would suggest they are lawmen, but there's something rundown and shady about them, so we're not sure how much to trust their point of view.) These are characters with a quest: They want to track down whoever they're following. And even though they don't seem to be the most savory folks, we're curious to find out if they do and what will happen. The author has also sprinkled some tantalizing half-revelations throughout this opening scene to keep us reading: the girl's bleeding foot, for instance. How did that happen? This plot is full of suspense.

Character: We get a quick sketch of each of the men: The leader with the silver-studded bridle, the gaunt man with the scarred lip, and the little man on the white horse. This isn't much description, but it's enough for us to distinguish the men. The silver bridle helps us remember that its owner is the leader. The scarred lip becomes a plot point when the gaunt man runs his hand over it; the fact that the author highlights that moment makes us feel like it's significant for the story. What gives us the idea that these men are rough and unsavory? For me, it was the behavior of the leader, who speaks "bitterly" and flashes "a quick intensity of rage" and then curses white horses. It seems like behavior unbecoming a lawman. Then again, frontier lawmen are complicated characters.

Dialogue: The characters speak to each other, and the author deftly reveals some of the plot through their dialogue.

Setting: The setting is very richly detailed, and directly so rather than between the lines. The author seems to be telling us that it will play a big role in the story, which makes sense considering its title.

Point of view: The point of view is third-person, by a narrator who seems to be all-knowing. However, as discussed, the anger and coarseness of the leader makes it hard to believe that these are law-abiding men simply after some "fugitives." Does a girl with a bleeding foot sound likely to be much of an evildoer? So, I was a little skeptical of the narrator's presentation of things. On the other hand, lawmen don't have to be saints, as I mentioned above.

You should know that H. G. Wells didn't set out with a five-column diagram in which he planned out the details of plot, character, etc. that he was going to put into his opening scene. But he knew that each would have to get at least a little attention if the story was going to feel well-fleshed and engaging.

Now, it's your turn. Here are some moments you might render in scene, if you're stuck:

1. A caravan of black sedans with tinted windows pulls up to a cemetery.
2. Soldiers serving in Afghanistan set out on a nighttime raid.
3. Your family sits down to dinner.

Let's flesh out one of these ideas together; say #1.

Plot: Why might a caravan of black sedans with tinted windows be pulling into a cemetery? Sounds like there's a burial of some kind. Who's died? A character of some kind. Maybe we don't yet know who. Maybe we need to figure out some of the story's other characters, or the setting, to give ourselves some clues. Let's jump to setting, since we have a bit of it already with the cemetery.

Setting: Questions to ask ourselves: Is this a cemetery in good condition, in a nice part of town, or rundown and poor? If we've got black sedans with tinted windows, I bet we're dealing with someone well-to-do. I haven't fully resolved my setting, but I'm feeling like brainstorming about my characters a little. Let's jump to the character department for a moment:

Character: So, an important person has died. Does that mean he had to have been a good person? Our "complicated character" lesson reminds us that the answer is no. What if this man was a mob kingpin? That would be interesting. My next thought takes me back to …

Plot: When Mafia kingpins die, they leave a big question: Who takes over? That shoots me back to …

Characters: What if this mob king has two sons, both in line for control of the organization. But instead of both being as criminal-minded as their father—let's have complicated characters!—one wants to inherit the business so he can expand it (typical), but the other wants to inherit so he can gradually shut it down (not typical). He's grown tired of having the family name associated with organized crime. Let's say he's a new father and he wants his daughter to grow up in a world where the last name—let's avoid stereotype and make them Irish instead of Italian—Busby stands for something other than murder and extortion. And to twist things even more, let's say that there's also Busby Sr.'s wife—the boys' mother. What does she want? On which side will she come down? Maybe that's a little mystery of the story. Something the reader doesn't know and will keep reading to find out.

Our characters also need physical descriptions. If the boys' mother's motives are mysterious, and her voice is likely to make an impact on what happens to the organization, then she sounds less like the mousy wife of a powerful man than a powerful woman in her own right. So I am imagining her as tall, attractive, perhaps wearing big sunglasses.

What about the boys? One could be Tommy, a typical Irish name—in our effort to complicate our characters, we don't want to go too far and have Irishmen named Boris, just to be different. The other son should have a less predictably Irish name. Monty? I like that name, short for Montgomery. Why not? Maybe he was Busby Sr.'s first son born in America, and Busby wanted to give him an American name. (A little bit of plot there.) Tommy is the brother who wants to expand the business, I've decided. He's younger, more impulsive, tall, thin. Monty is darker and more deliberate. (I'm just brainstorming here. If something in the story suggests that these characteristics should change, I will. These are just sketches toward the final drawing.)

~

I haven't filled out all of my 5 Essentials: I'm not sure about point of view, and the setting hasn't been fully fleshed out, but I've got enough on the page to want to get started. I believe everything else will come.

What you just saw is my approach to the problem you considered in the early weeks of this level: how to begin. I don't map out every little thing about the story, but I don't start myself with nothing more than a first line, either. I choose something in the middle, like what you saw above. I believe the rest will come—should come—while I'm writing.

In coming up with a scene of your own, refer back to your plot lessons from earlier this year. The first step is to come up with a situation for a story. The best kind of situation will have some kind of suspense, or a character on a quest. You might want to write out the situation in the middle of a notebook page, circle it, and draw five lines from the circle: plot, characters, dialogue, setting, point of view. You don't have to fill them in in order. Just sit with the situation and imagine something about it. Perhaps a setting will float up, perhaps you'll overhear a snatch of conversation. *Something* will occur to you. Then unravel the thread as we did in the example above.

Here's my stab, then, at a scene about the Busby family (525 words):

The long black centipede of cars maneuvered down Market Street [SETTING], the shopkeepers halting their business to nod fearfully at the hearse [PLOT] in the middle of the row of Town Cars.

"There goes Busby," they said.

"Busby's in that hearse," they whispered.

"Who's going to run things now?" they shook their heads. [PLOT]

"There hasn't been a death in that family in 40 years." [PLOT]

"I fear for this town." [PLOT]

"Last thing we need's a civil war."

In the Town Car directly behind their father's hearse sat the two young men likeliest to start the civil war the shopkeepers were referring to. Tommy Busby was tall, thin, pink as a baby. "Stretch," they called him because he passed six feet in junior high. Monty, the other, looked like he came from the Italians, not the Irish. He had dark hair and a stoop. Even his name—Montgomery, in full—was strange. No Irishman was ever named Montgomery, the locals whispered. What do you want, he didn't give it to himself, those who liked Monty said in return. But Monty was different, no doubt about it. [CHARACTER] Tommy wanted his father's business because he wanted to expand it. Monty wanted his father's business because he wanted to shut it down. He was sick of the Busby name being known for rackets and showing up on every crime list in the tristate area. When his daughter was born five years earlier, Monty had promised himself: By the time she goes to college, her last name won't mean much more than another to her classmates. To readers of the *Newark Star-Ledger*, however? To them, Busby would mean numbers and murder for a good long time to come. [PLOT]

"You know we'll have to talk," Tommy said, gazing out the window. [DIALOGUE]

"For God's sake, Tom," Monty said. "Man's bed is still warm."

"Meanwhile, you play your angles," Tommy said.

"There's a will, I'm sure. We'll do what it says. No matter what it says."

"He was senile for five years. Someone might as well say it. That will could be written in Gaelic."

"Fine. Mom will tiebreak."

"We could go evens."

"Someone has to be the boss, Tommy."

"You, of course. Always the boss, Monty." [PLOT]

"You want, we can ask the boys. Who do they want in charge."

"Forget it," Tommy said.

They were pulling up by the cemetery, a sprawling bluff overlooking an ugly part of Newark. [SETTING] Busby senior was fond of saying that his family came from the dumps of the city and they weren't above returning there in death. [SETTING TIED INTO CHARACTER.] The Busbys had a fenced enclosure of plots that stretched for a hundred yards. Two lions sat astride banisters at the entrance. A prickly rain began to fall from the sky. Both young men jumped out of their car to be the first to hover an umbrella over the head of their mother, Persephone Busby, the Greek-Irish goddess, the envy of all the boys down on Market Street. She might have to decide the fate of the business, and neither son wanted to find himself in the crosshairs of her disappointment.

～

As I was writing, I decided to set the story in Newark, a gritty town in New Jersey, my home state. That seemed to agree with the shady subject of the story. I needed to somehow convey to the reader who was in that hearse. I could have done it myself, as the author, in my all-knowing offstage voice, but as I was brainstorming, imagining that hearse pulling slowly through the midday streets, I saw—almost as in a movie—various shopkeepers turning around and falling silent as this revered and feared man made his final way through those streets. So I thought it might be effective to present him through their eyes. Meanwhile, they supplied some plot: that no one in the family had died in a long time, that there was fear of a conflict for control in the wake of Busby Sr.'s death. Then I set to describing the boys. Then they spoke to each other, each defending his viewpoint. I slipped in some plot information when I decided to make Tommy—younger, more cocky and impulsive—resentful of Monty's calmer demeanor. And so forth.

A note about genre: We'll talk about genre a lot more in future levels, but for now, I want you to note that this story is sounding a lot like a potboiler—the crime family, the tussle for future control. Doesn't this sound like an episode of a crime show or a mob movie? Different genres have different standards—for instance, crime films and books tend to spend less time on description and more on what happens next. Sometimes—though not always—they'll also be less selective about dialogue, because how something gets said is less important than what gets said, than getting information across to the reader (the contact didn't show; we were ambushed; etc.) Again, just something to keep in mind for now.

Your turn. Remember, this exercise isn't very different from things you've tried already. It just asks you to think about them in the same scene of fiction. Take things step by step, as outlined above. Write at least 500 words.

CHALLENGE EXERCISE

In preparation for next week's exercise, rewrite the scene, altering one crucial aspect—the basics of the plot, who the main characters are, the way in which they speak to each other, where the story takes place, or who's telling it.

PLAYING WITH THE VARIABLES IN A SCENE

Purpose: To continue practicing scene-writing by altering the elements of last week's scene.

This week, you're going to continue practicing scene-writing by tinkering with the scene you've created. Your mission this week will be to create five new versions of that scene, each one changing one (but only one) of the 5 Essential ingredients. So, if I was to do this exercise for my scene of the warring Busby brothers, the five rewrites might have these changes:

1. **Plot:** Tommy and Monty both want to dump Dad's business; it's their mother, Persephone, standing in their way. Or a bigger plot change: Busby Sr. was the governor of New Jersey. (Hence his honor funeral.) He left Ireland because of poverty, which Persephone was alive to see. She wants him buried in New Jersey, in a country that was good to the Busbys. Tommy (there's only one son in this version of the story) has been rediscovering his Irish heritage and believes Dad should be buried in Ireland. After the funeral's over, he intends to exhume his body and take it to Ireland for burial.

2. **Characters:** The plot remains the same, only the characters change. Perhaps there are no brothers. Perhaps there's a daughter and a mother, and they're in competition for the numbers empire.

3. **Dialogue:** I could make Tommy a very colloquial speaker of English ("Cry me a river, you jerk,") and Monty a self-important pontificator ("It would seem appropriate …"). Note that it's impossible to change dialogue without changing character as well.

4. **Setting:** Not Newark. Ireland.

5. **Point of View:** Monty narrates. Or Tommy narrates. Or—best of all—the deceased father narrates.

Please note that your job is to rewrite the scene five times, not only come up with five changes. I want you to see how the 5 Essentials overlap. Coming up with a different plot may affect what kind of characters you have. Changes in dialogue, as you saw up above, will force you to change your characters' personalities. And so on.

No challenge exercise this week, as you will have your hands full writing 2500 words. (Five segments of 500 words each.) It shouldn't feel as onerous as writing 2500 words from scratch since in each 500-word segment, you're changing only one element, though of course it may affect others. Here's my stab at a rewrite of my scene, with a change in the plot as above.

> The long black centipede of cars maneuvered down Market Street, the shopkeepers halting their business to nod at the hearse in the middle of all the Town Cars.
>
> "There goes Busby," they said.
>
> "The Guv," they whispered.
>
> "You see the Irish PM on the news? Wants him to be buried in Ireland. Only right. Native son and all that."
>
> "And what you think, Frank?"
>
> "I say Ireland's good for vacation, about all."
>
> "My kid wants to go."

"Mine, too, I tell you."

"What is it with them? I brought him here, and all he wants is go there."

"Some mistakes you got to learn on your own."

In the Town Car directly behind the hearse sat Governor Busby's two young sons. Tommy was tall, thin, pink as a baby. "Stretch," they called him because he passed six feet in junior high. Monty, the other, looked like he came from the Italians, not the Irish. He had dark hair and a stoop. Even his name—Montgomery, in full—was strange. No Irishman was ever named Montgomery, the locals whispered. What do you want, he didn't give it to himself, those who liked Monty said in return.

Monty belonged to that new generation of which the shopkeepers had spoken. Born into television, cars, Gameboys, then Xbox and iPhones. When was it enough? You could sit on Facebook all day long; numb fatigue was all you got out of it. When he was 14, Monty's father had sent him to a summer camp outside Dublin. Monty had been transformed: There was a pride in that soil. Less money but more pride. He didn't know how to put it other than that. But he believed that his father sending him there was a sign. Busby Sr. was too proud to return while alive to the country he'd left—left in poverty. But he wouldn't be too proud in death. Monty would make sure of that. He knew that's what his father secretly wanted, even if Tom said otherwise.

"Still thinking your crazy thoughts?" Tommy said, gazing out the window.

"For God's sake, Tom," Monty said. "Don't blab about it."

"Dig up Pa," Tommy snorted. "Ship him over there. I mean, just to think of it!"

"I tried talking to Mom. She won't hear of it."

"'That country did nothing for us. Don't you dare.'"

"Help me."

"Oh no, Boy-o. I ain't crossing Mother Fury."

"Well, at least keep your mouth shut."

"And I don't get a say? My pa too."

"You don't get a say because your vote's same as hers. I am telling you, he loved that place. Too proud to go back, but he loved it. You remember how much he asked after it when I got back. He wanted to know everything."

"I was a wee lad yet," Tommy said.

"Oh, don't talk like an Irishman," Monty laughed.

They were pulling up by the cemetery, a sprawling bluff overlooking an ugly part of Newark. Busby senior was fond of saying that his family came from the dumps of the city and they weren't above returning there in death. The Busbys had a fenced enclosure of plots that stretched for a hundred yards. Two lions sat astride banisters at the entrance. A prickly rain began to fall from the sky. The young men jumped out of their car to be the first to hover an umbrella over the head of their mother, Persephone Busby, the Greek-Irish goddess, the envy of all the boys down on Market Street. They were doing it for different reasons: Tommy because he was afraid of her, Monty because he didn't want her guard up against him. Neither son wanted to be on the wrong side of Persephone Busby.

Invariably, my plot shift changed the personalities of my characters. Tommy is more absent, less interested (more loving, too). Monty has a completely different set of priorities. Consequently, practically every word of their dialogue had to change, though the setting and point of view remained steady. This, as much as any lecture, should demonstrate the priority and interrelation of plot, character, and dialogue in a short story. Note, also, the new element of suspense: Will Monty or won't he? Will others find out? What will Persephone do in response?

Just as it was useful to see how much I needed to change to make the new plot work, it was fun to see how much I could manage to leave from the first version and still make sense under the new plot.

Remember: You'll need to end up with five different versions of the scene, each one shifting a single element.

ANOTHER SCENE FOR THE SAME STORY

Purpose: To make the 5 Essentials work through another scene using the same plot, character, etc.

This week, you will build on skills practiced over the last two weeks and write a second scene from the story you started two weeks ago. (Of course, you can choose to build on one of your modified scenes from last week instead of the original from two weeks ago.)

You may be on to my ruse: All this scenifying—to coin a word—is a way of working toward the semester-ending short story you will be writing next week. By the time you start next week's assignment, you will have at least two 500-word scenes, or half of the 2000-word story you will have to write.

You have your plot, your characters, and your point of view. These will remain the same in your second scene. However, this new scene may take place in a different setting and it will certainly have different dialogue. (Or no dialogue at all.) See below for my stab at a second scene for a story I might call "The Funeral."

Next scene in "The Funeral" (535 words):

> There was no stopping Tom. When they were kids and their father made them go up different streets shoveling snow to see who could make more cash, Monty stole off to borrow Timmy Rafferty's snowblower. It cost him

fifty bucks, but he had half the driveways on Lemonade Street plowed in two hours and two hundred dollars in his pocket. Tom didn't come home until five hours later, bowed like an old man under his shovel. He had cleared every single driveway on his street, and his pocket bulged with three hundred dollars.

Monty wasn't going to shoot his own flesh and blood. But Tom wasn't going to stop until one of them was on top. On Sundays, Tom always went to see Persephone, driving his personal car, a banged-up Oldsmobile unlikely to draw attention. He kept it in an old, ivy-covered warehouse guarded by an old watchman who had taught both boys how to shoot a bow when they were young.

Monty had to wait until the old man went off to the bathroom, then stole up to his thermos and crushed up half a sleeping pill. Remembering the old man's girth, he threw the rest of the pill in the tea. Then he returned to his hiding spot behind a hundred-year-old clutch of ivy. Ten minutes later, he heard snoring. He waited another 10 minutes to be safe, then crept past the old man. The warehouse smelled of car grease and old

leather. Monty banged around in the darkness until he found the car. The doors were open but not the trunk. Monty cursed Tom's strange habits, then jimmied the trunk, trying to leave no trace of his break-in. Then he emptied his briefcase into the trunk—wads of cash, address books, slips of paper with notes about how the numbers game worked. Then he walked out, stuffing a note in the old man's pocket: "For your safety, move to another state. Now."

The next afternoon, Monty was concealed behind Mrs. Frantz's azaleas, next door to his mother's, when Tommy pulled up. This most meandering of sons was always punctual with his mother, arriving at noon with a bouquet of

Gerber daisies, her favorite. His collar was popped and he wore spit-shined dress shoes. He wanted to impress.

Monty dialed with a leaden heart.

"911," the operator said.

"I would like to report a criminal action," Monty said, using a Spanish accent and trying for broken English.

"What is your location, sir?" the operator said.

"222 Lemonade," Monty said.

The operator paused. That address was known all over Newark.

"Please repeat," the operator said.

Monty was overcome by the full weight of his plan. He was sending his brother to prison so that he could have a free hand in liberating Newark of Busby, Inc. As he confirmed to the operator exactly where he was and exactly what the arriving police needed to look for, he chastised himself for a terrible slipup. He had taken care of everything, thought everything through—except for a fact so obvious he had missed it completely. The net that was about to ensnare Tom Busby was about to drag in his mother as well.

~

Your turn now.

CHALLENGE EXERCISE

Don't stop! Write a third scene.

Connect your two scenes with 100–200 words of telling. That is, tell us how the story got from the first scene to the next, or some kind of information the reader needs to know to jump from one scene to the next.

STORY UNIT: WRITING A STORY

WRITE A SHORT STORY

Purpose: To bring together the work of the last several weeks in a full-fledged short story.

This week, you will transform your two 500-word scenes (and perhaps the connective "telling" challenge exercise you did last week) into a 2000-word short story. If you find yourself going beyond 2000 words, that's fine. Just make sure you tell us a story that finishes what you started. The reader wants to know how things are going to turn out. Ask yourself whether all the threads you began to unspool in the opening 500-word segment from Week 15 are more or less addressed by the end. Stories don't have to resolve every loose end, but even when they don't, they need to provide the reader with enough of an idea of what to assume, in the absence of a concrete answer from the story. Otherwise, the reader is liable to feel cheated. Endings are tricky, and we'll practice them more formally in future levels of the series.

APPENDIX I

The Golden Goose

THERE was once a man who had three sons. The youngest of them was called Dullhead, and was sneered and jeered at and snubbed on every possible opportunity.

One day it happened that the eldest son wished to go into the forest to cut wood, and before he started, his mother gave him a fine rich cake and a bottle of wine, so that he might be sure not to suffer from hunger or thirst.

When he reached the forest he met a little old grey man who wished him "Good morning," and said: "Do give me a piece of that cake you have got in your pocket, and let me have a draught of your wine—I am so hungry and thirsty."

But this clever son replied: "If I give you my cake and wine I shall have none left for myself; you just go your own way." And he left the little man standing there and went further on into the forest. There he began to cut down a tree, but before long he made a false stroke with his axe, and cut his own arm so badly that he was obliged to go home and have it bound up.

Then the second son went to the forest, and his mother gave him a good cake and a bottle of wine, as she had to his elder brother. He too met the little old grey man, who begged him for a morsel of cake and a draught of wine.

But the second son spoke most sensibly too, and said: "Whatever I give to you I deprive myself of. Just go your own way, will you?" Not long after his punishment overtook him, for no sooner had he struck a couple of blows on a tree with his axe, than he cut his leg so badly that he had to be carried home.

So then Dullhead said: "Father, let me go out and cut wood."

But his father answered: "Both your brothers have injured themselves. You had better leave it alone; you know nothing about it."

But Dullhead begged so hard to be allowed to go that at last his father said: "Very well, then—go. Perhaps when you have hurt yourself, you may learn to know better." His mother only gave him a very plain cake made with water and baked in the cinders, and a bottle of sour beer.

When he got to the forest, he too met the little old grey man, who greeted him and said: "Give me a piece of your cake and a draught from your bottle; I am so hungry and thirsty."

And Dullhead replied: "I've only got a cinder-cake and some sour beer, but if you care to have that, let us sit down and eat."

So they sat down, and when Dullhead brought out his cake he found it had turned into a fine rich cake, and the sour beer into excellent wine. Then they ate and drank, and when they had finished the little man said: "Now I will bring you luck, because you have a kind heart and are willing to share what you have with others. There stands an old tree; cut it down, and amongst its roots you'll find something." With that the little man took leave.

Then Dullhead fell to at once to hew down the tree, and when it fell he found amongst its roots a goose, whose feathers were all of pure gold. He lifted it out, carried it off, and took it with him to an inn where he meant to spend the night.

Now the landlord of the inn had three daughters, and when they saw the goose they were filled with curiosity as to what this wonderful bird could be, and each longed to have one of its golden feathers.

The eldest thought to herself: "No doubt I shall soon find a good opportunity to pluck out one of its feathers," and the first time Dullhead happened to leave the room she caught hold of the goose by its wing. But, lo and behold! her fingers seemed to stick fast to the goose, and she could not take her hand away.

Soon after the second daughter came in, and thought to pluck a golden feather for herself too; but hardly had she touched her sister than she stuck fast as well. At last the third sister came with the same intentions, but the other two cried out: "Keep off! for Heaven's sake, keep off!"

The younger sister could not imagine why she was to keep off, and thought to herself: "If they are both there, why should not I be there too?"

So she sprang to them; but no sooner had she touched one of them than she stuck fast to them. So they all three had to spend the night with the goose.

Next morning, Dullhead tucked the goose under his arm and went off, without in the least troubling himself about the three girls who were hanging on to it. They just had to run after him right or left as best they could. In the middle of a field they met the parson, and when he saw this procession he cried: "For shame, you bold girls! What do you mean by running after a young fellow through the fields like that? Do you call that proper behavior?" And with that he caught the youngest girl by the hand to try and draw her away. But as soon as he touched her he hung on himself, and had to run along with the rest of them.

Not long after the clerk came that way, and was much surprised to see the parson following the footsteps of three girls. "Why, where is your reverence going so fast?" cried he; "don't forget there is to be a christening today;" and he ran after him, caught him by the sleeve, and hung on to it himself. As the five of them trotted along in this fashion one after the other, two peasants were coming from their work with their hoes. On seeing them the parson called out and begged them to come and rescue him and the clerk. But no sooner did they touch the clerk than they stuck on too, and so there were seven of them running after Dullhead and his goose.

After a time they all came to a town where a king reigned whose daughter was so serious and solemn that no one could ever manage to make her laugh. So the king had decreed that whoever should succeed in making her laugh should marry her.

When Dullhead heard this he marched before the princess with his goose and its appendages, and as soon as she saw these seven people continually running after each other she burst out laughing, and could not stop herself. Then Dullhead claimed her as his bride, but the king, who did not much fancy him as a son-in-law, made all sorts of objections, and told him he must first find a man who could drink up a whole cellarful of wine.

Dullhead bethought him of the little grey man, who could, he felt sure, help him; so he went off to the forest, and on the very spot where he had cut down the tree he saw a man sitting with a most dismal expression of face.

Dullhead asked him what he was taking so much to heart, and the man answered: "I don't know how I am ever to quench this terrible thirst I am suffering from. Cold water doesn't suit me at all. To be sure I've emptied a whole barrel of wine, but what is one drop on a hot stone?"

"I think I can help you," said Dullhead. "Come with me, and you shall drink to your heart's content." So he took him to the king's cellar, and the man sat down before the huge casks and drank and drank till he drank up the whole contents of the cellar before the day closed.

Then Dullhead asked once more for his bride, but the king felt vexed at the idea of a stupid fellow whom people called "Dullhead" carrying off his daughter, and he began to make fresh conditions. He required Dullhead to find a man who could eat a mountain of bread. Dullhead did not wait to consider long but went straight off to the forest, and there on the same spot sat a man who was drawing in a strap as tight as he could round his body, and making a most woeful face the while. Said he: "I've eaten up a whole oven full of loaves, but what's the good of that to anyone who is as hungry as I am? I declare my stomach feels quite empty, and I must draw my belt tight if I'm not to die of starvation."

Dullhead was delighted, and said: "Get up and come with me, and you shall have plenty to eat," and he brought him to the king's court.

Now the king had given orders to have all the flour in his kingdom brought together, and to have a huge mountain baked of it. But the man from the wood just took up his stand before the mountain and began to eat, and in one day it had all vanished.

For the third time Dullhead asked for his bride, but again the king tried to make some evasion, and demanded a ship which could sail on land or water! "When you come sailing in such a ship," said he, "you shall have my daughter without further delay."

Again Dullhead started off to the forest, and there he found the little old grey man with whom he had shared his cake, and who said: "I have eaten and I have drunk for you, and now I will give you the ship. I have done all this for you because you were kind and merciful to me."

Then he gave Dullhead a ship which could sail on land or water, and when the king saw it he felt he could no longer refuse him his daughter.

So they celebrated the wedding with great rejoicing; and after the king's death, Dullhead succeeded to the kingdom and lived happily with his wife for many years after.

APPENDIX II

The Golden Goose

THERE was once a man who had three sons. The youngest of them was called Dullhead, and was sneered and jeered at and snubbed on every possible opportunity.

One day it happened that the eldest son wished to go into the forest to cut wood, and before he started his mother gave him a fine rich cake and a bottle of wine, so that he might be sure not to suffer from hunger or thirst.

When he reached the forest he met a little old grey man who wished him "Good morning," and said: **"Do give me a piece of that cake you have got in your pocket, and let me have a draught of your wine—I am so hungry and thirsty."**

But this clever son replied: **"If I give you my cake and wine I shall have none left for myself; you just go your own way."** And he left the little man standing there and went further on into the forest. There he began to cut down a tree, but before long he made a false stroke with his axe, and cut his own arm so badly that he was obliged to go home and have it bound up.

Then the second son went to the forest, and his mother gave him a good cake and a bottle of wine, as she had to his elder brother. He too met the little old grey man, who begged him for a morsel of cake and a draught of wine.

But the second son spoke most sensibly too, and said: **"Whatever I give to you I deprive myself of. Just go your own way, will you?"** Not long after his punishment overtook him, for no sooner had he struck a couple of blows on a tree with his axe, than he cut his leg so badly that he had to be carried home.

So then Dullhead said: **"Father, let me go out and cut wood."**

But his father answered: **"Both your brothers have injured themselves. You had better leave it alone; you know nothing about it."**

But Dullhead begged so hard to be allowed to go that at last his father said: **"Very well, then—go. Perhaps when you have hurt yourself, you may learn to know better."** His mother only gave him a very plain cake made with water and baked in the cinders, and a bottle of sour beer.

When he got to the forest, he too met the little old grey man, who greeted him and said: **"Give me a piece of your cake and a draught from your bottle; I am so hungry and thirsty."**

And Dullhead replied: **"I've only got a cinder-cake and some sour beer, but if you care to have that, let us sit down and eat."**

So they sat down, and when Dullhead brought out his cake he found it had turned into a fine rich cake, and the sour beer into excellent wine. Then they ate and drank, and when they had finished the little man said: **"Now I will bring you luck, because you have a kind heart and are willing to share what you have with others. There stands an old tree; cut it down, and amongst its roots you'll find something."** With that the little man took leave.

Then Dullhead fell to at once to hew down the tree, and when it fell he found amongst its roots a goose, whose feathers were all of pure gold. He lifted it out, carried it off, and took it with him to an inn where he meant to spend the night.

Now the landlord of the inn had three daughters, and when they saw the goose they were filled with curiosity as to what this wonderful bird could be, and each longed to have one of its golden feathers.

The eldest thought to herself: **"No doubt I shall soon find a good opportunity to pluck out one of its feathers,"** and the first time Dullhead happened to leave the room she caught hold of the goose by its wing. But, lo and behold! her fingers seemed to stick fast to the goose, and she could not take her hand away.

Soon after the second daughter came in, and thought to pluck a golden feather for herself too; but hardly had she touched her sister than she stuck fast as well. At last the third sister came with the same intentions, but the other two cried out: **"Keep off! for Heaven's sake, keep off!"**

The younger sister could not imagine why she was to keep off, and thought to herself: **"If they are both there, why should not I be there too?"**

So she sprang to them; but no sooner had she touched one of them than she stuck fast to them. So they all three had to spend the night with the goose.

Next morning, Dullhead tucked the goose under his arm and went off, without in the least troubling himself about the three girls who were hanging on to it. They just had to run after him right or left as best they could. In the middle of a field they met the parson, and when he saw this procession he cried: **"For shame, you bold girls! What do you mean by running after a young fellow through the fields like that? Do you call that proper behavior?"** And with that he caught the youngest girl by the hand to try and draw her away. But as soon as he touched her he hung on himself, and had to run along with the rest of them.

Not long after the clerk came that way, and was much surprised to see the parson following the footsteps of three girls. **"Why, where is your reverence going so fast?"** cried he; **"don't forget there is to be a christening today;"** and he ran after him, caught him by the sleeve, and hung on to it himself. As the five of them trotted along in this fashion one after the other, two peasants were coming from their work with their hoes. On seeing them the parson called out and begged them to come and rescue him and the clerk. But no sooner did they touch the clerk than they stuck on too, and so there were seven of them running after Dullhead and his goose.

After a time they all came to a town where a king reigned whose daughter was so serious and solemn that no one could ever manage to make her laugh. So the king had decreed that whoever should succeed in making her laugh should marry her.

When Dullhead heard this he marched before the princess with his goose and its appendages, and as soon as she saw these seven people continually running after each other she burst out laughing, and could not stop herself. Then Dullhead claimed her as his bride, but the king, who did not much fancy him as a son-in-law, made all sorts of objections, and told him he must first find a man who could drink up a whole cellarful of wine.

Dullhead bethought him of the little grey man, who could, he felt sure, help him; so he went off to the forest, and on the very spot where he had cut down the tree he saw a man sitting with a most dismal expression of face.

Dullhead asked him what he was taking so much to heart, and the man answered: **"I don't know how I am ever to quench this terrible thirst I am suffering from. Cold water doesn't suit me at all. To be sure I've emptied a whole barrel of wine, but what is one drop on a hot stone?"**

"I think I can help you," said Dullhead. **"Come with me, and you shall drink to your heart's content."** So he took him to the king's cellar, and the man sat down before the huge casks and drank and drank till he drank up the whole contents of the cellar before the day closed.

Then Dullhead asked once more for his bride, but the king felt vexed at the idea of a stupid fellow whom people called "Dullhead" carrying off his daughter, and he began to make fresh conditions. He required Dullhead to find a man who could eat a mountain of bread. Dullhead did not wait to consider long but went straight off to the forest, and there on the same spot sat a man who was drawing in a strap as tight as he could round his body, and making a most woeful face the while. Said he: **"I've eaten up a whole oven full of loaves, but what's the good of that to anyone who is as hungry as I am? I declare my stomach feels quite empty, and I must draw my belt tight if I'm not to die of starvation."**

Dullhead was delighted, and said: **"Get up and come with me, and you shall have plenty to eat,"** and he brought him to the king's Court.

Now the king had given orders to have all the flour in his kingdom brought together, and to have a huge mountain baked of it. But the man from the wood just took up his stand before the mountain and began to eat, and in one day it had all vanished.

For the third time Dullhead asked for his bride, but again the king tried to make some evasion, and demanded a ship which could sail on land or water! **"When you come sailing in such a ship,"** said he, **"you shall have my daughter without further delay."**

Again Dullhead started off to the forest, and there he found the little old grey man with whom he had shared his cake, and who said: **"I have eaten and I have drunk for you, and now I will give you the ship. I have done all this for you because you were kind and merciful to me."**

Then he gave Dullhead a ship which could sail on land or water, and when the king saw it he felt he could no longer refuse him his daughter.

So they celebrated the wedding with great rejoicing; and after the king's death, Dullhead succeeded to the kingdom and lived happily with his wife for many years after.

POETRY

WHAT TO WRITE ABOUT

WHAT DO POETS WRITE ABOUT?

Purpose: To acquaint you with how poets have handled a variety of subjects in their poetry.

It's difficult to discuss what poets have chosen to write about without discussing how they've done it, so we will touch on that as well. But our main focus in this first four-week unit is: "I know I want to write a poem, but what should I write about?" Let's see how a handful of poets throughout history have done it.

Your assignment this week is to write at least 100 words in your notebook discussing what each of the following poems is about. Your challenge exercise is to write another 100 words for each one of these poems that focuses not on what the poem is about, but other distinctive aspects of the poem: The rhythm (does it rhyme? jump off the tongue as you read it out loud? sound like a song? like a piece of prose?); language (are there interesting descriptions or comparisons? are the words very precise, specific, and even technical?); are the lines short or long? (what effect does this create on the reading of the poem?); and anything else that comes into your mind.

My own brief analysis of each of the poems follows, if you need a little help getting started. But your reading of the poem doesn't have to agree with mine.

The Owl

Alfred, Lord Tennyson

When cats run home and light is come,
And dew is cold upon the ground,
And the far-off stream is dumb,
And the whirring sail goes round,
And the whirring sail goes round;
Alone and warming his five wits,
The white owl in the belfry sits.

When merry milkmaids click the latch,
And rarely smells the new-mown hay,
And the cock hath sung beneath the thatch
Twice or thrice his roundelay,
Twice or thrice his roundelay;
Alone and warming his five wits,
The white owl in the belfry sits.

2

Worldly Place
Matthew Arnold

Even in a palace, life may be led well!
So spake the imperial sage, purest of men,
Marcus Aurelius. But the stifling den
Of common life, where, crowded up pell-mell,
Our freedom for a little bread we sell,
And drudge under some foolish master's ken
Who rates us if we peer outside our pen,
Match'd with a palace, is not this a hell?
Even in a palace! On his truth sincere,
Who spoke these words, no shadow ever came;
And when my ill-school'd spirit is aflame
Some nobler, ampler stage of life to win,
I'll stop, and say: "There were no succour here!
The aids to noble life are all within."

Piccadilly Circus at Night
D. H. Lawrence

When into the night the yellow light is roused like dust above the towns,
Or like a mist the moon has kissed from off a pool in the midst of the downs,

Our faces flower for a little hour pale and uncertain along the street,
Daisies that waken all mistaken white-spread in expectancy to meet

The luminous mist which the poor things wist was dawn arriving across the sky,
When dawn is far behind the star the dust-lit town has driven so high.

All the birds are folded in a silent ball of sleep,
All the flowers are faded from the asphalt isle in the sea,
Only we hard-faced creatures go round and round, and keep
The shores of this innermost ocean alive and illusory.

Wanton sparrows that twittered when morning looked in at their eyes
And the Cyprian's pavement-roses are gone, and now it is we
Flowers of illusion who shine in our gauds, make a Paradise
On the shores of this ceaseless ocean, gay birds of the town-dark sea.

#4 # When You Are Old
William Butler Yeats

When you are old and grey and full of sleep,
And nodding by the fire, take down this book,
And slowly read, and dream of the soft look
Your eyes had once, and of their shadows deep;

How many loved your moments of glad grace,
And loved your beauty with love false or true,
But one man loved the pilgrim soul in you,
And loved the sorrows of your changing face;

And bending down beside the glowing bars,
Murmur, a little sadly, how Love fled
And paced upon the mountains overhead
And hid his face amid a crowd of stars.

#5 # Impression de Voyage
Oscar Wilde

The sea was sapphire coloured, and the sky
Burned like a heated opal through the air;
We hoisted sail; the wind was blowing fair
For the blue lands that to the eastward lie.
From the steep prow I marked with quickening eye
Zakynthos, every olive grove and creek,
Ithaca's cliff, Lycaon's snowy peak,
And all the flower-strewn hills of Arcady.
The flapping of the sail against the mast,

The ripple of the water on the side,
The ripple of girls' laughter at the stern,
The only sounds:—when 'gan the West to burn,
And a red sun upon the seas to ride,
I stood upon the soil of Greece at last!

#6

A Farm Picture
Walt Whitman

Through the ample open door of the peaceful country barn,
A sunlit pasture field with cattle and horses feeding,
And haze and vista, and the far horizon fading away.

#7

Mending Wall
Robert Frost

Something there is that doesn't love a wall,
That sends the frozen-ground-swell under it,
And spills the upper boulders in the sun;
And makes gaps even two can pass abreast.
The work of hunters is another thing:
I have come after them and made repair
Where they have left not one stone on a stone,
But they would have the rabbit out of hiding,
To please the yelping dogs. The gaps I mean,
No one has seen them made or heard them made,
But at spring mending-time we find them there.
I let my neighbour know beyond the hill;
And on a day we meet to walk the line
And set the wall between us once again.
We keep the wall between us as we go.
To each the boulders that have fallen to each.
And some are loaves and some so nearly balls
We have to use a spell to make them balance:
"Stay where you are until our backs are turned!"

We wear our fingers rough with handling them.

Oh, just another kind of out-door game,

One on a side. It comes to little more:

There where it is we do not need the wall:

He is all pine and I am apple orchard.

My apple trees will never get across

And eat the cones under his pines, I tell him.

He only says, "Good fences make good neighbours."

Spring is the mischief in me, and I wonder

If I could put a notion in his head:

"Why do they make good neighbours? Isn't it

Where there are cows? But here there are no cows.

Before I built a wall I'd ask to know

What I was walling in or walling out,

And to whom I was like to give offence.

Something there is that doesn't love a wall,

That wants it down." I could say "Elves" to him,

But it's not elves exactly, and I'd rather

He said it for himself. I see him there

Bringing a stone grasped firmly by the top

In each hand, like an old-stone savage armed.

He moves in darkness as it seems to me,

Not of woods only and the shade of trees.

He will not go behind his father's saying,

And he likes having thought of it so well

He says again, "Good fences make good neighbours."

What are these poems about?

1. "The Owl" is, quite obviously, at its most literal, about an owl. As the morning world awakes from the slumber of night, the owl continues its motionless vigil. Perhaps it's this solidity and quiet authority that the author tries to evoke by repeating certain lines. The repetition creates a feeling of grandeur, constancy, and solidity. (Note that the repetition functions in two ways: 1) in both stanzas,

he repeats the fourth line, different in each stanza; 2) he concludes both stanzas with the same two lines.[4]) Notice, as well, the rhymes in the poem.

2. "Worldly Place" is about an idea: What has meaning in life—wealth, or inner nobility? As you'll learn when we study some common forms next year, "Worldly Place" is a sonnet. (Can you map out which lines rhyme with which?)

3. "Piccadilly Circus at Night" is a poem about the place of the title, but it expands to take in a theme related to "The Owl": human vs. animal nature. So it actually has more similarity in subject to #2, which also grapples with an idea.

4. "When You Are Old" is a love poem, addressed to the loved individual.

5. "Impression de Voyage," like #3, is a poem about place, though more literally so.

6. "A Farm Picture" is a poem about a place, and about nature—and a good example of how a brief poem can say a great deal—but perhaps it's most distinctive here because it dispenses with the rhyme scheme that has been a staple of the first five poems. Line breaks are "easy" when it comes to rhymed poetry—you break on a rhyme. With poets like Whitman, a precursor of the modern shift to poetry without perfect rhyme, the line break becomes a whole new kind of tool. Can you say why Whitman might have decided to break his three lines where he did?

7. For a bigger challenge, can you say why Robert Frost might have broken the lines where he did in this poem about the relationship between neighbors in a country place? Note, as well, the repetition of the poem's key line: "Good fences make good neighbours." Did it have a different impact the second time around? Your answer should consider the fact that its second usage is at the very end of a poem, a place that naturally amplifies whatever is placed there. It's our last contact with the poem, the last thing in our minds.

---

4 A stanza is a group of lines, separated from other stanzas by a blank line.

MORE CHALLENGE EXERCISES

1. Pick up a copy of *Sleeping on the Wing* by Kenneth Koch and Kate Farrell. This book presents a selection of poems by great poets across periods and countries, along with explanatory essays—written in plain language—by the authors: a great introduction to several wonderful poets, along with some guidance on what they write about and how. (Another rich source is "Subjects for Writing," the opening section of *The Poet's Companion* by Kim Addonizio and Dorianne Laux.)

2. Create your own version of *Sleeping on the Wing*: Pick a poet out of the seven featured above (or another altogether) and read at least 10 more poems by him or her. Fill 500 words in your notebook discussing this author's style, subject matter, etc. This will be of assistance to you next year, when you are asked to write a poem imitating a favorite poet.

FINDING MAGIC IN THE ORDINARY

Purpose: To learn how to say something unusual—and poetic!—about something ordinary.

Some poets write about everyday things: The trees outside as they change color during the autumn; or the expression on a friend's face as she hears bad news; or a memory, like the last time the circus came to town. Such poets believe that the everyday is magical, if you look closely enough. They focus on ordinary moments, looking closely until they notice something extraordinary about them. They believe that the rest of us move too quickly through everyday life, failing to notice the magical in the everyday.

This week, you will try to do something similar. **Your assignment is to write 10 lines of poetry about something ordinary.**

STEP 1:

Your first step is to find that something ordinary to focus on.

Is there something that you think is special, or unusual, but everyone else thinks is ordinary? It could be an object, such as the birdhouse outside your window. Everyone in your family know it's there. Maybe your dad put it out there, and a sibling

of yours regularly replenishes the feed, but no one sits watching it for hours, noticing the habits of the birds that visit. So you can write about that.

Or <u>how</u> about focusing closely on someone in your family? You and your siblings and your parents interact all the time, but how about observing one of them more closely than you usually do? What if you remain in the kitchen after breakfast, and watch your mother or father as they move through the household's chores? What is your mother thinking about as she washes the dishes and gazes distractedly out the window? How do her hands look as they clean the plates?

STEP 2:

Once you've picked something to focus on, you need to observe it very closely for a while: Spend several hours looking out at the birdhouse, or several hours with your mom in the kitchen. Take lots of notes in your notebook. These notes can simply record what's happening, as in a log or a diary, though even these are likely to send your mind drifting constructively:

> Mom is washing dishes. She's wearing that apron that we got her for Christmas, with a photograph of the family. It's stained all over the place. It's funny, I can probably trace the meals we've had over the last several months on that apron. There's some burgundy color from the kidney beans in the meatloaf, and there's some cream from the mac and cheese.

You see? You started writing down what was in front of you, and your imagination drifted off, using the apron as a kind of puzzle, holding within it the story of this family's meals since Christmas.

STEP 2B:

Another thing you could do in your notebook, in addition to noting your direct observations, is to make yourself come up with several comparisons for what you're seeing.

Examples:

- Hummingbirds alight on the feeder, stab the seeds with their beaks, and flit off, all in a second. It reminds me of a concert of classical music on television, the conductor's hands flitting above the notes. The music was a little boring, but I remember the conductor's hands flying above the stand with his notes like a bird's wings.

- Mom gazes out the window, squinting to make something out in the distance. It's like she's an explorer trying to sight land. What is she looking for? What is she looking to "discover"?

STEP 3:

What else do poems feature, in addition to observations and imaginative comparisons? They feature careful word choice. As you observe the scene in front of you, try to record the proper terms for what you're seeing. If you don't know what kind of bird is stopping by the birdhouse, you might look it up in an online database of birds. (Or you can simply decide that it is a hummingbird or a robin. Being inaccurate factually is less important here than being specific.) Is there a technical name for what these birds eat? "Feed"? "Seeds"? Of what kind of wood is the birdhouse made? "Pine"? You should find out. And so on.

STEP 4:

Your last step, before starting to work on the 10 lines of your poem, is to underline, circle, or highlight those things that you know you'd like to include in the poem. It might be a general direction for the poem—discussing Mom's apron as a map of the family's meals—or an image you love (the conductor's hands flitting like a bird's), or simply something amazing you noticed, such as the way two hummingbirds seem to communicate with each other. These will become the anchors of your poem.

STEP 5:

It's time to start writing. At this point, you don't know how many stanzas you should have, where your lines should end, or whether any lines will rhyme. That's okay. The first draft is an information dump: You're going to put down some information from your notes, and see where it takes you. Let's say you'll write about your mom at the sink.

> I watch my mom at the sink. [Simple enough, right?
>   It's great because the reader knows immediately
>   where we are.]
> Through the mesh [specific] of the window,
> she squints at Maugahunk Ridge [specific]
> as if she's sighting land ["sighting" is technical,
>   making us think of an explorer]
>
> What are you looking for, Mom?
> Are you looking at yourself at my age?
> Or who I will become when I'm yours?
> Or maybe you are mapping out dinner.
>
> I can map every dinner since Christmas
> on your apron, your Christmas gift
> with its funny image of us.
>
> The kidney beans from the
> meatloaf for Grandmother's birthday,
> the cream from Charlie's mac and cheese.
>
> Mother, you are my compass.

～

So, this poem turned out to be 15 lines instead of 10. If you're exceeding the limit, don't worry about it. Same if you're falling short of the 10 lines, but only if you have a good reason for the poem to end sooner.

This poem got more interesting as I started writing it. If you remember, in the last unit of the fiction section, I presented you with my method for writing stories: I brainstorm a fair amount, but don't map out every detail. That gets fleshed out in the course of the writing itself. Same thing here. I knew I'd mention Mom looking out the window, and the apron, but I certainly didn't know or plan for the poem to have a theme of discovery, exploration, maps, etc. That only emerged in the writing. It was only as I was thinking of the actual lines that I realized that "Or maybe you're thinking of dinner" can become "mapping out dinner," continuing the theme started with "sighting." And then "I can map every dinner..." flowed naturally from there, leading us to the poem's final line, which also deals with navigation, which has already become a small theme of the poem. In the end, it became a poem about Mom looking out of the window while washing dishes, but also about something larger. It's hard to say exactly what that something larger is, but we can agree that it has something to do with home and direction in life—where our harbors are, so to speak. This is the something larger and universal and extraordinary that poets believe poems about ordinary things can bring us to.

If someone asked you, "Do you love your mom?" You'd say, "Of course, I do." And if this person asked why, you'd waste no time in saying "She loves us, and takes care of us, and is a loving person." But you'd agree that answer would be a lot less striking and affecting than how the same sentiment emerges in a poem like the one above. This is the beauty of poetry: It can say movingly and profoundly the things that we all feel and sometimes struggle to find a way to express adequately. Also, it isn't corny.

A brief note about stanzas and line breaks in the poem: I didn't stress too much about this in my first draft. I could hone these aspects when I revise. Some of my choices seem logical, I hope. The first stanza proceeds by clauses—"I watch Mom at the sink./ Through the mesh of the window,/she squints at Maugahunk Ridge/as if she's sighting land." These lines are all more or less of the same length. That felt natural to me. The poem then moves into questions for Mom, which felt like they should form a new stanza. Each new question makes a new line. The poem's next thought—about being able to read the apron, and where the apron comes from—appears in the next stanza. The fourth stanza is about the poem's next thought—what the narrator can map out on the apron. The last stanza only consists of one line and is meant to startle the reader a little bit because it's so short. It carries the poem's ultimate message.

Your turn.

CHALLENGE EXERCISES

1. To prep yourself for this exercise, spend a day envisioning your life as different than it is, as something fantastical, and your everyday life's other elements—your parents, your chores, your clothes—as elements of the same invented drama. You can imagine yourself as a member of a royal court, or an explorer in the Arctic, or a fashion designer in New York. As you go through the day, try to keep the narrative of this "other life" going in your head, imagining picking up clothes off the floor of your room as actually picking up design samples off the floor of your design studio in New York. It's as if your "real life" is merely a theater stage, and if you pull back the curtain, your "invented life" as a fashion designer/explorer/ member of a royal court will emerge. This is a mental exercise that may get you in the habit of seeing more than is there—the skill that this week's assigned poem is meant to exercise.

2. During the week of this exercise, write down in your notebook 10 ordinary objects/visions/experiences like the one profiled above. For each, come up with a general direction for a poem about the ordinary thing in question. By "general direction," I mean broadly what the poem will be about. It doesn't have to be any more specific than "Mom standing at the sink looking at something and her apron with traces of all the meals she has made for us, a poem about how much I love her."

3. Don't stop at 10 lines. Write a full poem—say, at least 20 lines.

WRITING POETRY ABOUT THE EXTRAORDINARY

Purpose: To turn last week's assignment on its head and write some poetry about something outlandish.

The poet not only finds the magical hiding behind the everyday. She also notices the magical—period. As human beings, we tend to try to explain away the unconventional. If the moon doesn't rise some night, you can bet that most people will try to explain it away as nothing special; perhaps the cloud cover is heavy, is all. But the poet relishes the unusual event, fixates on it, explores its meaning and consequences—perhaps by writing a poem about what a world without a moon would be like, or by recalling a long-ago walk by moonlight.

This week, you will look for the out-of-the-ordinary. A poet isn't merely an observer: she's an inventor, too—so the extraordinary situations you decide to write about can be real or invented. Examples of both:

REAL SUBJECTS

1. A book I read recently mentions an accident on a massive ship in the Pacific that was carrying hundreds of tons of tuna. The tuna fell into the ocean, and soon

enough, thousands of sharks had surrounded the ship to gobble it up. Thousands of circling, hungry sharks—that's something you don't see everyday.

2. A man walking down the middle of the highway instead of the sidewalk.

3. Your lawnmower breaks down and your dad dredges up, from the depths of his toolshed, a rusty scythe of the sort used to mow grass before mechanized agriculture.

4. A cheetah. It sounds pretty simple, but most of us don't get to see cheetahs that regularly. A sighting would be a pretty rare, precious thing. A poem describing its movement might sound simple, but because so few of us have ever observed a cheetah in motion, I think it would be fascinating. And I bet that describing the cheetah's motion might bring you to all sorts of other interesting thoughts.

5. Watching the vapor trail of an airplane dissipate very slowly on a windless day. This is borderline: ordinary, perhaps, but if you've ever patiently observed it happening, you know it's quite amazing, and something many people don't see—or pay attention to.

INVENTED SUBJECTS

1. A world in which all food tastes the same.

2. A world in which nobody dies.

3. A chip in the mind enables owners to speak a foreign language or to have the memory of having been in a place they've actually never visited.

4. A tree that takes off into the stratosphere like a spaceship, the nesting birds assuming the responsibilities of the astronauts.

5. A world in which all homes stand on stilts and, at night, while their inhabitants sleep, go walking. (Where do they go? Why? What do they say to each other?)

PART 1

Come up with five real and five invented extraordinary visions that could serve as subjects for poems. In the case of the invented five, you will have to use your imagination. In case of the real five, you will have to use your observation skills. Look around yourself—at home, in your neighborhood, in town, on a drive if your family happens to go somewhere. The out-of-the-ordinary or nonstandard is all around us.

PART 2

Write 10 lines of poetry about this extraordinary sighting. An idea for a poem starts to become a poem through the application of craft: line breaks, stanzas, rhythm, and so on. We'll be practicing that throughout this year. For now, just focus on getting your impressions about the extraordinary vision to look like a poem.

Here's what a 10-liner about the extraordinary visions in some of my examples from the previous page or two could focus on:

Real #1: A poem about the circling sharks could focus on the visual spectacle of all those swirling, massive bodies; that is, it could be heavy on description. Or their aggressiveness could put the author in mind of some aspect of human nature, like the tendency to act in groups and not think independently.

Invented #3: Albert Einstein said that signing a letter recommending the creation of the atom bomb was "the great mistake in [his] life." This poem could be about the inventor who invented the chip and now regrets it, since people use it to sit on their couches instead of going anywhere. Or it can describe one such mind trip to a foreign place. Or it can describe the experience of being able to form words and meaning in a language one does not know.

To come up with the actual lines, follow the process from last week.

Here is an example of how a 10-liner might read:

> The day must have been windless
> Because the vapor trail
> In the sea-blue sky
> unwound as slowly as
> day becomes night.
>
> As a child, I would have seen
> dinosaurs become violins
> become kingly staffs
> before becoming
> nothing.
>
> As a child,
> I would not have looked up.
> "Look where you're going,"
> Was the refrain of my childhood.
> And look where I've come.

∾

Once again, I broke the rules and exceeded the 10-line assignment. What is this poem about? It's about noticing the incredible shapes an airplane's vapor trail makes in the blue sky as it unravels into nothing. But then the poem uses the experience to compare what the narrator might have seen up there as a child. So, even though the poem is most obviously about watching a vapor trail recede in the sky on a cloudless day, it's also about getting older and the human sense of wonder.

The **stanzas** proceed by subject. The first one deals with a description of the vapor trail. The second describes what the narrator would have seen up there as a child. The third links the two.

LINE BREAKS

Take the first stanza as a line of prose:

> "The day must have been windless because the vapor trail in the sea-blue sky unwound as slowly as day becomes night."

How to break up this line into poetry? To me, there are natural stopping points in the reading of this line—places to take a quick breath. "The day must have been windless" is one. "Because the vapor trail" is another. "In the sea-blue sky" is the next. In the fourth and fifth lines, I decided to create a wee bit of suspense by cutting off the fourth line after "as," hoping the reader would rush on to the next line to find out: "… as what?"

By the time I was finished with the first stanza, I saw that I had five lines. That made me try to keep to five lines in the second stanza as well, as well as the third, so there would be a pattern, lending the poem a certain rhythm.

Notice that the second stanza tries to imitate the experience of airplane vapor unraveling into nothing by making its lines shorter and shorter. They talk about one thing transforming into something smaller and then something smaller before becoming … nothing.

DESCRIPTION

I really did watch the vapor trail from an airplane dissipate into nothing on a recent morning. So many things happen so quickly in our world nowadays—e-mail, downloads, news—that it was almost difficult to find the patience to watch something so slow. (This would be a fine subject for a poem, too.) The other thing that I noticed was how difficult it was to track the change of the shapes from one thing to another. If someone showed me, side by side, photographs of the vapor trail five minutes apart, they would have looked completely different. But watching the trail change from one thing to another, it was almost impossible to record the change. At that moment, I recalled that I have always thought the same thing about dusk—the way day turns into night. So I used that image as a comparison.

Notice also that I didn't settle, simply, for blue sky. The poet has to dig deeper and find a more precise, vivid word. (We will practice this later in the year.) I thought about more imaginative ways to describe the blue sky. I could have said "powder-blue" or "navy-blue" but those are pretty common usages as well. So I tried to think of an object as blue as the sky. It was then that I thought of the "sea"—an unexpected way to describe the sky, but it sticks in the mind.

The second stanza is full of comparisons; that's its point. There's a little echo between the experience of watching the vapor trail turn into shapes and writing a poem full of comparisons.

Some of the thinking above may seem somewhat advanced, but I just wanted to show you the wonderful complexities that can go into writing a poem. It's really meant to set your imagination, and your verbal talents, free. You can use poetry to explore worlds unseen by anyone else, detail experiences unexperienced by anyone else, describe the sky as like the sea or a blue pupil or a lilac flower, and much else. Don't try to imitate anything I've done above in your 10-liner. Just use it, if you can, to understand that you can write about anything, in any way you want. There are some guidelines you can use to make your poems better—more vivid, more affecting—and we will be exploring them throughout this level. But for now, just feel free to roam.

CHALLENGE EXERCISE:

Find five published poems that describe something extraordinary. Discuss with your mentor 1) what's extraordinary about the subject, and 2) how the poet chooses to handle it. One example to start you off is "Tar," by C. K. Williams, available online, about a nuclear disaster. To find others, read around. Look up poems by the poets in the first week of this exercise, or root around the sites Poets.org and Poemhunter.com, which offer many examples of poems.

FROM THEMES TO SITUATIONS

Purpose: How to improve ideas for poems by focusing abstract subjects into concrete situations.

Let me tell you a story:

In graduate school, I took a class with a writer named David Lipsky. For our first class, David assigned us a short story by the fiction writer Michael Chabon. The story, "A Model World," is about a student who plagiarizes a paper from an old book. "What is this story about?" David asked during the class. "Integrity," I said confidently. "No," David said. "It's about a guy who decides he's going to plagiarize his paper out of an old book."

In a way, both David and I were right. But the big difference between our answers is that mine was an abstraction and his was concrete. David was saying that Michael Chabon didn't set out to write a story about integrity. He set out to write a story about a guy who decides to plagiarize, which, unavoidably, ends up being a story about integrity. If he'd set out to write a story about integrity, he would've ended up with all sorts of vague, sweeping generalizations, which is far less interesting. As readers, we respond to specifics, because they enable us to imagine ourselves in the protagonist's situation. Poems work similarly.

Concrete is always better than abstract in fiction and poetry because they thrive on the specific. Why? Let me ask you what you feel when I say the word "love." Quick, what pops into your mind? Maybe Valentine's Day, maybe a movie you saw? Okay. What do you feel if I say "grizzly bear covering her cubs"? Whatever you feel—and it may be difficult to put into words—I bet it's going to be a lot stronger and more focused than the vague, generic associations you have with an abstract word like "love."

Abstractions are generalities. An abstraction might mean two completely different things to two different readers; a problem for an author who is hoping to create a specific image in the reader's mind. What's more, remember that fiction and poetry are not like movies: as a reader reads, he doesn't have visual cues from the screen to help him along. All the visual aids have to come from the imagination. How can the imagination get working if it's not sure what to imagine—Valentine's Day, or the movie *Shakespeare in Love*, or a man pulling out a chair for a woman as they sit down to dinner at a restaurant, or a boy giving a girl a flower? Those are very different situations, you'll agree.

All this applies just as much to the process of deciding what to write a poem about. Very often, we will be moved to write poetry (and by the way, this goes just as much for fiction) by some broad, abstract feeling. "I want to write a poem about love." Or "I want to write a poem about my family." Or "I want to write a poem about my friends." Or "I want to write a poem about my house."

The problem with these ideas is: Where to begin? You could say a thousand things about your family, your house, your friends. Now, imagine that instead of writing a poem about love, you decide to write a poem about picking flowers in a field for someone you love. It seems small—just one little thing, how can it encapsulate everything you want to say about love? But the trick with poetry is that a poem about picking flowers in a field for someone you love is likely to say a lot more about love than a poem about love. It's like an illusion.

Can you come up with concrete alternatives to the three abstract topics below my example?

Abstract	Concrete
A poem about my family	<u>A poem about how early my dad rises to go to work</u>
A poem about my friends	_____
A poem about my house	_____
A poem about love	_____

Your assignment this week has several parts. The first is to translate five out of the eight abstractions supplied by me, below, into concrete situations that could serve as more effective subjects for poems, just like above. Your "translation" can be as short as a sentence fragment or as long as several sentences—however long it takes you to "translate" the broad abstraction into something specific. You don't have to write the poem or a scene or anything like that. Just tell me what this new, more concrete poem would be about. That should usually fit into a sentence fragment, like the example below.

Here's an example, using one of the three abstractions above.

A poem about my house	A poem about watching the stars from my roof while everyone sleeps

PART 1

Here are the abstractions. **Translate them into concrete situations:**

1. A poem about fear   _____
2. A poem about laziness   _____
3. A poem about gratitude   _____
4. A poem about danger   _____
5. A poem about destruction   _____
6. A poem about gentleness   _____
7. A poem about deception   _____
8. A poem about generosity   _____

The best way to start translating these abstractions is to ask yourself: What kind of fear? Where? Who? Think about the last time you experienced fear, or heard about something that had scared someone else. Find a horror novel in the library. Walk through the house at night with the lights off. Ask a friend or a parent about the last time s/he was scared. All these experiences will work to make your idea of the abstraction in question more specific.

PART 2

The second part of your assignment is to come up with five abstractions of your own. Remember, the world isn't divided into "abstract" and "concrete." There are gradations of abstraction and concreteness. "Flowers" is fairly concrete, but "azaleas" is even more so. "Sunset" is fairly concrete, but "a palette of streaking pinks, yellows, and violets" is even more concrete. So, "flowers" and "sunset" can be perfectly fine abstractions. Anything that can be made more specific can work as an abstraction.

And don't limit yourself to feelings, such as "greed" or "love." "Con" is an abstraction (what kind of con?); so is "football" (what about football?). Colors are abstractions. "Blue" is abstract but "blue bookshelf" is not. Numbers are abstract. "Four" is abstract but "four finches" is not. As long as you can ask, "What kind of _____?" You've got yourself an abstraction.

Your turn. Come up with five abstractions. Abstractions tend to be one-word—sunset, greed, football, blue—because as you start adding words, you start adding specificity. But if you happen to come up with a sentence-length abstraction, that's fine, too.

    1.

    2.

    3.

    4.

    5.

PART 3

Now take those five abstractions and translate them into five more concrete situations, as you did in Part 1.

CHALLENGE EXERCISE

1. Write a 10-line mini-poem about one of your 10 concrete situations.

2. Keep a log of every abstraction you hear or read in a week. Come up with a concrete situation for each. (Politicians, for instance, love abstractions because they sound nice but are vague enough for few to object, and make it very difficult for the politicians to be held to their words.)

WORD CHOICE

EVERY WORD HAS FIVE SENSES

Purpose: To get up close and personal with words by using the Five Senses.

Last week, you translated abstractions into concrete situations. This week, we're going to take the same challenge further. You'll get even closer to abstractions by coming up with personalities for them using the Five Senses.

You should get used to the idea that words have personalities. They are as alive as you want them to be. And it pays to get acquainted with those personalities, so the words you have at your disposal are words that will stay with your reader long after he or she has finished the poem.

This week, you'll come up with abstractions, just like you did last week, and ask yourself:

- What does the word look like?
- What does the word feel like?
- What does the word sound like?
- What does the word smell like?
- What does the word taste like?

Of course, the answers to these questions are going to be imaginative rather than logical. Of course, "confusion" doesn't smell like anything in the "real" world. But in the world of poetry, it does. (By the way, abstractions like "confusion" are a great way of practicing your word-personality skills because they don't come with any ready associations, the way a concrete word like "dove" would. This is exactly what makes them bad to use in a poem, but perfect for this exercise.)

So, let's come up with a personality for "confusion." Here's my stab at it:

- Confusion looks like … a foggy morning.
- Confusion smells like … oatmeal burning on the stove.
- Confusion sounds like … the bells of a church going off with a deafening roar.
- Confusion tastes … bitter.
- Confusion feels like … a jellyfish.

Can you guess how these associations might have arisen in my mind? Confusion is the state of being lost, uncertain, between answers. At least that's how I process it. And so the concrete comparisons that floated up for me have to do with a lack of clear boundaries—fog, the shapelessness of a jellyfish. The other answers are less literal, being more generally negative—a bitter taste, a loud noise. (However, a loud noise is literal, too; confusion, after all, is the state of being pulled in different directions, mentally, and a noise is distracting in a similar way.) You'll also notice that I could have done better with the taste assignment: "Bitter" is quite abstract.

By the way, confusion doesn't have to be negative. If confusion smells to you like a Japanese garden, all those delectable options competing for your attention, so be it!

Your turn. **Come up with five abstractions, just like you did last week. Then, for each, draw up a personality, as I did above.** If you're stuck, remember that your answers don't have to be literal. If you're trying to figure out the personality of a word like "persistence," just say the word out loud and sit for a moment. Be alert, to catch any associations that arise in your mind. I bet it will be easiest to answer the question "What does it look like?" The first image that pops into my mind is of a giant man, for some reason wearing a wrestler's outfit, trying to lift a car off the ground. How's that for odd? But off-center associations like that are exactly why we do exercises like this one. We can all look in the dictionary to find out

what "persistence" means. A poet's job is to bring the abstraction alive in a poem in an original way: "The Wrestler's Persistence."

But the exercise becomes tougher when you have to answer less literal questions like "What does it sound like?" You really have to use your imagination here. To me, persistence sounds like something shrill, the sound of a poorly oiled door or rusty gears changing, over and over. There's something repetitive about persistence to me, hence the repetition of the sound I imagine—if I had to explain it.

There's no reason that persistence couldn't sound to you like an airplane nosing gracefully through the sky. To one person, persistence is strained, stubborn, pushing against constant obstacles. To another, it's a smooth glide, forward motion and progress, always streaming ahead. Both are equally valid. But you'll agree they create very different sensations in the reader, which is why you should almost never use a word like "persistence" in a poem. You have to specify what kind of persistence.

Okay, your turn. Start by coming up with five abstractions, below. Remember that not only feelings like "confusion" and "persistence" are abstract. Colors are abstract—blue means a black-and-blue to one person, and a cloudless sky to another—as are seasons. And the abstraction doesn't have to be a noun: generic adjectives like "fast" and generic verbs like "to support" also would work.

  1.
  2.
  3.
  4.
  5.

Now, for each abstraction, finish the thoughts below.

  1. Looks ...
  2. Sounds ...
  3. Smells ...
  4. Tastes ...
  5. Feels ...

CHALLENGE EXERCISES

1. Answer as many Five-Sense questions as you can for the 26 letters of the alphabet: "A" looks like a tower; sounds like an arrow pinging through the air, etc.

2. Do a Five-Senses association for five words you don't know.

3. Write a mini-poem (10 lines or thereabouts) about an abstraction, using as many of your Five-Sense associations as possible. It could be about the fact that confusion smells like burned porridge ("The burned smell of confusion …"), or it could incorporate the Five-Sense associations while imagining confusion as a living creature.

SUBSTITUTION!

Purpose: To improve the words that we use in our poems.

In poetry, finding the perfect word for what you want to say is even more critical than in prose. A poem uses far fewer words than a short story, so each has to do a lot more work. Put differently, a poet has much less room to say everything he wants to say, so he has to pick the best words for what he's trying to get across. What makes one word better than another?

As we discussed last week, concrete words (beech) are more effective than more general ones (tree). They conjure a more specific image in the mind of the reader.

Other words simply sound like they belong more than their alternatives. Take the word "mellifluous." It means "producing a sound pleasant to the ear." But you could have guessed that simply from the way the word flows along, like a ribbon or a river. The word sounds like its definition.

Other words work better because of the rhythm they produce. Compare "the dove that sits above the eaves" to the "dove that sits above the mantelpiece." The second example is clunkier, isn't it? In the first example, you have rat-tat-tat rhythm: "Da-DUM da-DUM da-DUM da-DUM. The DOVE that SITS a-BOVE the EAVES. (Emphasis on the capitalized parts of the words.) Not so in the second example, where the long and clunky "mantelpiece" changes the rhythm entirely.

So, words matter. To give you a small example: Here's a mini-poem I wrote about insomnia—the ailment of being unable to fall asleep at night—personifying it as you did your abstractions last week:

Insomnia, you ancient dog.
By my bed every night,
Immobile, collapsed, a pile of flesh,
even when I send you away.

I throw the newspaper, the ball, the bone.
But your loyalty to me
Goes against even
Animal instinct.

You stay put, studying me with pitiful eyes,
As loving as death.

Let's focus on the first line:

Insomnia, you ancient dog.

It's not a bad line. But can we replace "ancient" with something better? Better need not mean "fancy" or "complicated." In fact, I might go with "old." Why? It's a plainer word than "ancient" but I like it because it's as short as "dog"—and as short as "you," for that matter—and "you old dog" rolls off the tongue in a way "you ancient dog" doesn't. "Ancient" drags on a little bit, sort of the way "mantelpiece" did above. One other thing I like? There's something almost chummy about "you old dog," whereas "you ancient dog" is formal. If insomnia is like an unwanted friend who comes to visit every night, "you old dog" captures the mix of familiarity and frustration with this visitor better, I think. So, there's first-hand evidence that, sometimes, simpler is better. (Remember, though, that "old" isn't some kind of "correct" answer here. A case could be made for another replacement—but it would take the line in another direction.)

So, this week, your job will be to take my poem about insomnia and find better alternatives for the adjectives, images, and verbs blanked out on the next page:

Insomnia, you _____ dog.
By my bed every night,

_____, _____, _____,
even when I _____ you away.

I throw the newspaper, the ball, the bone.
But your loyalty to me
Goes against even
Animal instinct

You stay put, studying me with _____ eyes,
As loving as _____.

Let's review:

- Line 1: Come up with an alternative for the adjective "old."
- Line 3: Come up with a different adjective for "immobile," a different adjective for "collapsed," and a different description for an image like "pile of flesh."
- Line 4: Find a different verb for "send."
- Line 9: Come up with an adjective to replace "pitiful."
- Line 10: Find another image for "death."

Above, you don't have to be literal. Try to approximate the feeling aroused by a word like "old" as much as trying to come up with a strict synonym for it. For instance, "grimy" could work: "you grimy dog." "Grimy" doesn't mean "old," but dogs can be grimy and it has that frustrated resentment that someone suffering from insomnia might have.

What did you come up with?

CHALLENGE EXERCISE

Pick up a poem that you love, blank out all the comparisons, adjectives, verbs, and nonspecific nouns. (But keep the specific nouns—those words that don't have superior substitutes—like banana, chicken bone, conscientious objector, nuclear plant, tar.) Then replace the blanked-out words with superior alternatives, just as in the week's exercise.

FILL IN THE BLANK/ POETIC MAD LIBS

Purpose: To find that perfect word.

This week, we're going to focus even more closely on finding the perfect word in a line of poetry. Credit for this exercise goes to the poet Ted Kooser, who mentions it in his book *The Poetry Home Repair Manual*. Below you will find 10 fragments of poetry. Five of them are mine, and five are from published poetry. **Each one will have a missing word, which it will be your job to fill.**

The original words follow at the end of this exercise. Your job isn't to guess them, but to find replacements that make sense to you. The idea here is to isolate a single word and think hard about which might be the best: the most powerful, vivid, and memorable. To increase the challenge of the exercise, limit yourself to a single word.

In the second part of this exercise, erase your choices and come up with a different answer *that changes the meaning of the original.*

Example, using #1 from the list below.

1. From the bluff, we made shelves
   of palms over our eyes,
   and called out wishful sightings,
   knowing all we saw was _____.

Part 1: "knowing all we saw was *brush*"
Part 2: "knowing all we saw was *bodies*"

Your turn.

1.   From the bluff, we made shelves
of palms over our eyes,
and called out wishful sightings,
knowing all we saw was _____.

2.   Aye cap'n, tis a pity
You won't let us sing a ditty.
Let us _____ our spirits, chief;
The sea is bleak and life is brief.

3.   Youth is _____ on the young, they say.
So is adulthood on adults.

4.   Fear not, my faithful _____;
We'll ride no more tonight.
The sun is low, the dust is high,
We'll wait until it's bright.

5.   I propose a revision
        to the idea that poems are boring.
        Perhaps we are fearful
        of enjoying the _____?

6.   Row, row, row your boat
        Gently down the stream

        _____, _____, _____, _____

        Life is but a dream.

It isn't hard to guess the original here, so please don't use "merrily." You should feel free, however, to use the same word four times, or, for a challenge exercise, come up with four different ones. Also up to you whether they will be adjectives or not, or a mix with other sentence parts.

7.   A flock of sheep that leisurely pass by,
        One after one; the sound of rain, and bees
        Murmuring; the fall of rivers, winds and seas,
        Smooth fields, white sheets of water, and pure sky;
        I have thought of all by turns, and yet do lie _____![5]

8.   To be, or not to be: that is the _____.[6]

Same note as "Row, row your boat": Surely you know what goes here. Your answer can't be "question."

5 From William Wordsworth's "To Sleep."
6 From William Shakespeare's Hamlet.

9. The old piano plays an air,

    _____ and slow and gay;

    She bends upon the yellow keys,

    Her head inclines this way.[7]

10. Tyger, tyger, burning bright

    In the forests of the night,

    What immortal hand or eye

    Could frame thy fearful _____? [8]

ORIGINALS FOR 1–10:

1. grief
2. cheer
3. wasted
4. steed
5. darkness
6. merrily
7. sleepless
8. question
9. sedate
10. symmetry

CHALLENGE EXERCISE

Play this game with other forms of writing: A random sentence from the book you're reading right now; from the newspaper on the kitchen table; from the cereal box. Ask your mentor to blank out the word before you see the sentence.

---

7 From James Joyce, "The Twilight Turns From Amethyst." "Air" is an old word for "tune" or "melody."

8 From "The Tyger" by William Blake. Note that lines 3 and 4 don't have to rhyme. "Tyger" is an old spelling of "tiger."

KENNING

Purpose: To find new ways to say the same things.

Imagine a dictionary that defines words not by explaining what they mean, but by rephrasing them as metaphors. (Metaphors are direct comparisons, such as "The lake is a bowl.") This would be a dictionary of *kennings*. Kennings come to us from Old Norse, an ancient Scandinavian language. Old Norse poets were big fans of kennings, and when you look at the selection of kennings below—culled from a great list on Wikipedia—you'll agree that they add a nice epic touch. (You'll also notice that the Old Scandinavians did a lot of fighting. "Blood," in particular, seems to have inspired quite a few kennings.) For our purposes, they're a great way to practice our poetic language skills. Coming up with kennings tests our skills with metaphor, description, synonyms, and linguistic flexibility in general. It also, quite simply, forces us to see the same old things in new ways.

- battle: spear din
- blood: slaughter dew, battle sweat, wound sea
- death: sleep of the sword
- fire: bane of wood
- sea: whale road
- serpent: valley trout

- ship: wave steed
- sun: sky candle
- sword: wound hoe and (my favorite!) onion of war
- war: weather of weapons
- wind: tree-breaker

Shall we come up with a couple of kennings a little more suited to our lives today?

What about …

- table: food pedestal
- stairs: paralyzed escalator
- airplane: engine-bird

With "table," I went for a straightforward description, so to help yourself, a good question to ask might be: "What is its function?" With "stairs," I kept thinking that stairs look like an escalator, only they don't move. And that's how I got to "paralyzed escalator." So, there, the question that led me to an answer was: "What does it look like?" The kenning for "airplane" combines 1 and 2 in that it's both a description based on a comparison ("bird") and incorporates one of the airplane's functions ("engine.")

Your assignment this week is:

Part 1: Come up with kennings for 10 nouns with which I'll supply you.

Part 2: Come up with kennings for 10 nouns of your own choosing.

Your kenning can be longer than two words. For instance, snow can become "white skirt of the earth." A tree can become "the ground's green hair."

PART 1

Come up with kennings for the following 10 items:

1. Book
2. Computer
3. Wall
4. Wind
5. Clothing
6. Spaceship
7. Leaves
8. Smile
9. Aggression
10. Congress

PART 2

Your turn. For Part 2, come up with 10 words of your own, and then with kennings for each of them.

1.
2.
3.
4.
5.
6.
7.
8.
9.
10.

CHALLENGE EXERCISES

1. Take a poem that you've written and rewrite it, changing as many nouns as possible into kennings. Sounds pretty epic, no?

2. Take a published poem that you love and do the same thing.

RHYME REDUX

Purpose: To practice word choice under another kind of restriction: sound.

A great way to close out the word choice unit and preview the form/sound unit that follows is to talk about rhyme. What is rhyme if not word choice under pressure, right?

In brief, a rhyme scheme is marked by letters of the alphabet. The sound at the end of the first line is given the letter *a*; any line that ends in the same or a similar sound also gets the letter *a*. So, if the second line rhymes with the first, it's also marked by an *a*. If it has a different sound, it's marked by a *b*. (And any line whose final sound resembles the second one's gets a *b*, too.) And so on. So, to use as an example some of the rhyming stanzas from the Mad Libs exercise from two weeks ago:

2.   Aye cap'n, tis a pity (a)
    You won't let us sing a ditty (a)
    Let us cheer our spirits, chief; (b)
    The sea is bleak and life is brief. (b)

4.   Fear not, my faithful steed; (a)
    We'll ride no more tonight. (b)
    The sun is low, the dust is high, (c)
    We'll wait until it's bright. (b)

7.   A flock of sheep that leisurely pass by, (a)
       One after one; the sound of rain, and bees (b)
       Murmuring; the fall of rivers, winds and seas, (b)
       Smooth fields, white sheets of water, and pure sky; (a)
       I have thought of all by turns, and yet do lie (a)
       Sleepless! …[9]

This week, you will choose one of two exercises: to write your own poem according to a rhyme scheme you arrange in advance, or to fill out a poem whose rhymes have been provided by me. The one you don't choose will be your challenge exercise.

9 From William Wordsworth's "To Sleep."

Here's mine:

_____ still (a)
_____ will (a)
_____ bury (b)
_____ merry (b)

_____ clone (c)
_____ alone (c)
_____ wary (b)
_____ tarry (b)

_____ slight (d)
_____ might (d)
_____ fairy (b)
_____ reliquary (b)

_____ control (e)
_____ soul (e)

Some guidance/loopholes:

- You can switch around any rhymes that have the same letter.
- You can substitute one (but only one) pair of rhymes (for instance "control" and "soul"), replacing it with a pair that rhymes the same sound ("ol/oul").
- The lines don't have to be the same length.
- Feel free to place punctuation before or after the rhyming words I've provided.
- As in all poems, don't feel like each line has to have a complete thought.

The alternative is to come up with a rhyme scheme of your own before writing the poem, and try to fulfill it. Here are some examples:

1. Alternating rhyme (four lines in each stanza): **abab cdcd efef ghgh** …
2. Couplet-style (two lines in each stanza): **aa bb cc dd** … (It won't surprise you to learn that triplet-style is to rhyme **aaa bbb ccc** …)
3. Enclosed rhyme: **abba cddc effe** … (That is, the *a*'s enclose the *b*'s, the *c*'s enclose the *d*'s, and so on)

4. Simple 4-line: **abcb defe** … (The second and fourth line of every stanza have the same sound.)

Of course, you can come up with a rhyme scheme of your own (as I did in my poem up above, **aabb ccbb ddbb ee**, the *b* like the chorus of a song, coming back every once in a while). But make sure that you have at least five rhyming pairs in your poem, and that it has at least 14 lines, like mine above. (If you calculated that this means I'm giving you two pairs of lines that don't have to rhyme, you're absolutely right. Use them wisely!) Rhyme is easiest with stanzas of an even number of lines (4, 6) but there's no reason you can't have creative rhyme in a stanza of five lines, too.

CHALLENGE EXERCISE

As mentioned above, do the exercise you didn't do in the lesson.

FORM AND SOUND

REPETITION

Purpose: To understand how repetition affects the sound of poetry.

Poems can and ought to be like music, where repetition is the norm. Whether you're repeating letters and sounds (b-, bl-, etc.), full words ("dream"), or phrases ("if you will,") the recurring sound becomes like an incantation. Think back to Week 2 of this level, when I repeated navigation-related images in a poem about one's love of his mother. Weren't they more powerful each time they surfaced, in a new context? And those were just images! Imagine the even more powerful echo created by the recurrence of the same sounds, like a chorus from a song sticking in your mind long after you've turned it off.

Your assignment this week is to write some lines of poetry where every line begins with the same word(s) or ends with the same word(s). The poem can consist of as many lines and stanzas as you like.

The idea of patterning in poetry has a long and very rich history across cultures, about which you can find out more if you do the challenge exercise. If you don't, we'll explore it together in the levels to come.

You'll note that starting every line with the same word(s) is probably easier than finishing each line with the same words. Compare this stanza pattern—

> Tell me …
> Tell me …
> Tell me …
> Tell me…

with the other option in this exercise, which might look something like this (I chose the word "time" at random):

_____ time
_____ time
_____ time
_____ time

It is much simpler to finish each one of the lines beginning "Tell me" with a different phrase than to figure out what sentences would all end with the word "time."

Regardless of which you attempt, you should try to make sense with your poem. If you're wondering why, it's because the mandated repetition injects such a nonrational dose of sound focus into the poem that a little sense in the content is just what's needed for balance.

Here are examples of both:

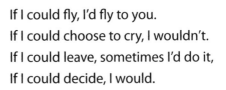

If I could fly, I'd fly to you.
If I could choose to cry, I wouldn't.
If I could leave, sometimes I'd do it,
If I could decide, I would.

If I could bear, I'd bear it all,
If I could take your share, I would.
If I could take you with me,
If I could make you come along.

If I could lick the moon,
If I could poke the sun,
if I could drink the sea,
If I could, I would.

If I could be a stork, I would.
If I could be a wolf, I would.
If I could be a jet, I would,
If I could be alone, I wouldn't.

~

They say that all it takes is time.
Give it some time.
All in good time.
What heals all wounds? Why, time.

From time to time,
I want to take time
And thrash it well a time
or two, cursed time.

Time,
time,
time,
time.

Ahead of time,
behind the time,
I keep time,
and bide my time.

~

Discuss with your mentor what the poems sounded like to you. Read them aloud. Then have them read aloud to you. Jot down any sensations, impressions, observations. Does the repeated word ring in your head like a church bell when the poem is over? Did your or your mentor's reading of the poem accelerate as you went on? I find that happens a lot when I am reading the same word over and over in a poem. What else did you notice? Do you see the power of repetition to affect the sound of the poem? If not, find words to substitute—you're a pro at that—for every use of the repeated word. Doesn't that sound like a different poem?

The second exercise was much tougher for me. "Time" was a good choice for the final word because it's general enough for many kinds of lines to end in it. But it was a lucky choice also in that the challenge to end 16 lines of poetry in the same word is very confining (in a good way) so that by the end I was feeling as cramped as the person in the poem.

The first exercise was fun! (Okay, almost. It's an exercise, right?) As in many other cases, I didn't plan what to say. Simply, I wrote the first line—"If I could fly, I'd fly to you"—and went from there. Not every line in the poem fits easily, in terms of meaning, with every other line, but it doesn't have to. I hope you'll agree that the reader comes away from it with a general—if vague—sense of loss, distance, privation, and longing. In that, it's a decent example of how a poem can conjure an aura or mood without being easily understandable on a literal level.

What should you choose as your mantra for repetition? (If you can't decide how many lines/stanzas your poem should have, let's use our standby: A four-stanza poem, each stanza consisting of four lines.) A great guideline for starting words is: Use word(s) that beg an answer:

- If it wasn't for …
- The first time I …
- If I could …
- The last time I …
- I love … I hate …

By the way, if you end up choosing a paired locution such as "I love … I hate …," it's fine to alternate repeating lines:

> I love …
> I hate …
> I love …
> I hate …
> I love …
> I hate …

If you're struggling, repeat only the first line of each stanza:

> If I could fly,
> Then birds would walk
> And rhinos talk.
>
> If I could fly,
> Then …

As for end-word repetition, brainstorm to find words general enough that many lines of poetry could end in them. They could be general in that they are abstract ("time"), have many literal meanings ("will"), or have many metaphorical meanings ("game").

Examples:

- time
- fate
- wheel
- work
- alone
- light
- grace
- home
- game
- chance

Ironically, words that I deemed too abstract in other concepts can work very well here, because only something that broad can accommodate 16 lines of poetry. You just try to end 16 semisensible lines of poetry in a very specific word like "curtain."

CHALLENGE EXERCISES

1. If you did the starting-word repetition, do the end-word repetition poem, and vice versa.

2. Do you have a favorite song? Look up the lyrics online and underline every repetition. Do the same thing for a favorite poem. Underline not only repeating words (obviously, you can skip articles, prepositions, etc.) but repeating phrases, and, for extra-extra credit, repeating sounds (-ts, -bl, -ch, -mn, etc.). This will be of great use to you in an upcoming lesson on sound.

3. Songs rely on repetition far more consistently than poems do, so you may have to go through a couple of poems before you find one that actually relies on it. If you're stuck, here are some poems that make use of repetition:

- "Do not go gentle into that good night," by Dylan Thomas
- "The Hollow Men," by T.S. Eliot
- "The Charge of the Light Brigade," by Alfred, Lord Tennyson (who is already familiar to you from Week 1)

LINE BREAKS

Purpose: To learn more about line breaks through the ultimate challenge: one word per line.

Line breaks are the points at which lines of poetry end, and one of the great distinctions between poetry and prose. Poets use them like a tool to create an effect on the reader—just as they use description, word choice, and so on. To grasp in concentrated form just how much of a difference line breaks can make, this week, we're going to do the ultimate line-break exercise: a poem consisting of one word per line. This lesson was inspired by the wonderful poet Kenneth Koch—I mentioned his book *Sleeping on the Wing* in the challenge exercises to the first lesson. He discusses one-word-per-line poems as well.

If you've come across the poetry of William Carlos Williams, it often comes close to this: Only several words per line. Look up some classic examples online: "The Red Wheelbarrow," "Apology," "Between Walls."

This week, we're taking the idea even further.

Let's review some line-breaks basics. Line-breaks aren't some invented device, designed to make a poet's life more complicated. A poet experiments with sound, and you'll agree that the next two excerpts read very differently:

You old sleepless beast

vs.

You old sleepless
beast

The first example is closer to prose—it elicits few questions. The second, however, makes us rush to the second line, to find out: "You old sleepless" what?

You'll remember, as well, that line breaks require a slight pause. The first example above leads us to pause in a natural spot. The second also requires a pause, just in a spot where you wouldn't normally do it, between the adjective and the noun. This changes the sound of the poem. It doesn't make it better or worse, necessarily, just different.

To get really sensitized to how line breaks work and what they can achieve for a poem, **we're going to practice writing a poem that has no more than a single word in each** of its lines. Like many times this year, the number of lines and stanzas is up to you, though if you need an instruction, **aim for 4 four-line stanzas, totaling 16 lines.** (That means your poem will have 16 words.)

Here's an example:

> Insomnia,
> you
> old
> dog.
>
> By
> my
> feet
> like
>
> a
> clock.
> Even
> when
>
> I
> beg
> you,
> Go.

You'll notice this is a slight rearrangement of my insomnia poem from earlier this year. You can feel free to work with something you've written or come up with something new. But do restrict yourself to this week's assignment: one word per line.

Some things worth noticing: My first stanza ends on a complete sentence. The second carries over into the third, and the third into the fourth. Simply, notice that this creates different effects. A single line consisting of a complete sentence reads differently than a line consisting of a fragment—compare "the old sleepless clock finally rests" with "the old sleepless"— and the same thing goes for a stanza.

Now let's discuss the effect of using no more than one word per line. What do you think of the poem above? Here was my experience, after reading it out loud. (Remember to pause at the end of each line, no matter how unnatural that might seem. For me, pausing at the end of each line became more natural the further in the poem I read.)

The first line is declarative; it announces our subject. I hoped the reader would be a little curious to hear what the second line would say about that subject. The second line introduced some suspense: "you." You what? The third line prolonged the suspense; it's descriptive but doesn't answer all our questions: "old what"? I am interested partly because this poem is clearly going to describe insomnia, a physical condition, as an object. The fourth line finally grants some relief to the suspense: "dog."

The rest of the lines proceed by a similar logic. "By" what? "By my" what? Relief: By my feet. But "like" what? "Like a" what? Relief: clock. Again: "Even when" what? Relief: Even when I beg you. "Beg you" to what? Relief: Go.

Suspense isn't the only purpose of line breaks. By stretching a sentence or a fragment over multiple lines (or stanzas)—or not—the poem creates subtle feelings: of rushing along, of meandering, of stopping short.

Compare the excerpts on the following pages:

1.   Stop.
        No
        more.
        Tired.

        Weak.
        Annihilated.
        Exasperating
        Foolishness.

        Desist.
        Refuse.
        Deny.
        Conscientiously,

        Object.
        Resist.
        Refuse.
        Deny.

2.   Down
        the
        river's
        silty

        ribbon
        the
        sun's
        first

        cold
        ray
        seeks
        the

direction
of
the
day.

3.   Is
there
news?
And

now?
And
now?
I

can't
abide
the
roar

of
all
this
silence.

~

The first example seeks to defeat the purpose of the exercise. It avoids run-ons by end-ing most of its sentences at the ends of its lines. Also, it works against the natural rush of lines that carry no more than a single word by slowing them down with long, labo-rious words. The poem feels much longer than 16 lines—doesn't it?—especially when compared to #2 and #3?

The second example takes full advantage of the form. It describes something easygoing and meandering, and does so in an easygoing and meandering style, each line gently proceeding to the next, creating suspense but not urgency, just as the sun's ray gently climbs over the river.

The third example also has forward momentum, but it's a desperate, urgent, addled momentum. It rushes rather than meanders: the form, it can be said, is as nervous and jumpy as the subject. The lines are not **end-stopped** as they are in the first example. They're a hive of activity, just like the narrator's brain.

Finally, it's your turn to take over. You've seen many variations of what line breaks can achieve. What will yours?

CHALLENGE EXERCISES

1. Don't stop at one 16-word poem. Write five, each one creating a different effect.

2. Your second challenge exercise is to write a poem with two words per line—no more, no less. Two words per line may have seemed restricting before this exercise, but doesn't it seem so liberating now by comparison with a one-word-per-line poem?!

INTRODUCTION TO METER—THE HAIKU

Purpose: To start our syllable-counting practice in preparation for next year.

As you may remember from your introduction to this level, meter refers to the rhythm of a line of poetry. It depends, more than anything else, on two things:

1. The number of syllables in a line
2. Which syllables get emphasized as the line is read out loud

Put another way, ME-ter comes DOWN to the NUM-ber of SYL-la-bles, and WHICH of those get EM-pha-sized when we SPEAK.

Poets who write free verse—that is, the majority of modern poets—don't rely on meter a great deal. But until the 20th century—well into it, in fact—meter was the standard. And if nothing else, the creative restrictions it imposes are a great way to sharpen one's poetry skills.

There's an old legend: A new couple just moved into a very cramped home. They couldn't afford anything bigger, but they couldn't squeeze into what they had. They decided to seek a wise man's counsel: "What should we do?" they asked him.

"Do you have chickens?" he asked them. They said that they did. "Bring them inside the house," the wise man told them. The newlyweds didn't understand his logic, but decided to obey. They brought in the chickens, but now it was even more cramped! They returned to the wise man to ask for more advice.

He asked them: "Do you have pigs?" They answered that they did. "Bring them inside the house," the wise man said. And so on it went: cows, horses, etc. Finally, the newlyweds were living in a house so cramped they could barely take a step without knocking into some animal.

In desperation, they took a final trip to the wise man, and said: "This can't stand! It's ten times worse than it was in the beginning. Please help!" The wise man said: "Now take all the animals and return them to the yard." The newlyweds did it. And all of a sudden their home felt as spacious as a palace.

Telling this story was a very elaborate way of saying: Restrictions double the sense of freedoms when we remove them. As Robert Frost is famous for saying, writing poetry that doesn't rhyme—that is, without the creative restrictions imposed by rhyme, which make you work harder for word choice—is like tennis playing without a net. Robert Lowell is another renowned poet who subjected himself to the constraints of various rhyme schemes, syllable counts, and accent because working without them was, in a sense, too easy. (Interestingly, Lowell came to feel that taking this too far—achieving technical perfection—was meaningless without feeling, like an ice skater who executes every jump perfectly but clearly doesn't have her heart in the performance. But we're in no danger of approaching that problem just yet.)

This week, we'll only dip our toes in the water and focus strictly on syllable-counting. A great way to do so is to practice some haiku. Haiku is a Japanese form of poetry. Haiku have only three lines. But each line must have a very specific number of syllables, no more and no less. The first line must have five; the second, seven; and the third, five once more. Here's an example by Matsuo Basho, one of the masters of the Japanese haiku, composed in the late 17th century:

> Furu ike ya
> kawazu tobikomu
> mizu no oto

In the Japanese, the poem has five syllables in the first line, seven in the second, five in the third. Here's the English translation (by Robert Aitken):

> The old pond;
> A frog jumps in —
> The sound of the water.

I wonder if we can make an English-language haiku out of this translation—which currently has three syllables in the first line, four in the second, and six in the last—without changing the meaning:

> The e-ter-nal pond
> A frog jumps in the wa-ter.
> The sound of the splash.

I really had to put my Synonym Cap on in Line 1. Even good ol' "an-cient" from Week 6 wouldn't sub for "old" here because we need an extra two syllables, not one. I achieved the necessary seven in Line 2 simply by extending it (and borrowing a key word with a precious two syllables from Line 3). The third line was a little tricky,

Line 2 having stolen some of its goods. What could mean the same thing as water? Our "kenning" practice came in handy here. Isn't "splash" just another way of saying "water," and spending one less syllable to boot?

This week, you will write five haiku of your own. To narrow down the number of decisions you'll have to make, I'll lead you toward topics:

1. My first day at [fill in the blank].
2. When it's raining and gray, I [fill in the blank].
3. I wish I was [fill in the blank].
4. The best place I've ever been to.
5. When I become older, one thing I'll do regularly is [fill in the blank].

CHALLENGE EXERCISES

1. Expand your syllable-counting to other domains. Count the syllables in a sentence one of your parents speaks this week; in a textbook you're using; in a television commercial; in an instruction manual. Do at least five.

2. Transform the five sentences in challenge exercise #1 into haiku.

A LECTURE ABOUT SOUND

Purpose: To learn how to listen closely to our words.

> A lecture about sound
> by a man named Goold Brown
> (though the first time I saw it
> was in a book by a poet)

A little rhyme to get you started there. This week, we'll talk a bit about sound. The first part of our lesson will be a lecture courtesy of the 19th-century grammarian Goold Brown. (I owe thanks to the American poet Mary Oliver, in whose poetry handbook—titled, appropriately enough, *A Poetry Handbook*—I first came across this lecture.)

In the second part of our lesson, we will try to apply some of what we learned to published poems. Before we launch into Goold Brown's lecture, however, turn the page for a poem by Mary Oliver herself, just because she's a wonderful poet.

In Praise of Craziness, of a Certain Kind

Mary Oliver

On cold evenings
my grandmother,
with ownership of half her mind—
the other half having flown back to Bohemia—

spread newspapers over the porch floor
so, she said, the garden ants could crawl beneath,
as under a blanket, and keep warm,

and what shall I wish for, for myself,
but, being so struck by the lightning of years,
to be like her with what is left, that loving.

~

As you read the following lecture, don't try to memorize what Goold Brown is saying, especially the terminology. For now, just try to make sense of the points he's making. Say the sounds out loud. Come up with words that illustrate what he means. Try to understand how the feelings he ascribes to that sound might make sense. After all, what he's doing for individual sounds, you've already done for whole words, in the Five Senses exercise in Week 5. You may find it handy to read the lecture several times. On first read, it will probably sound like a foreign language, but if you keep trying again and again, its secrets will begin to open up to you.

A LECTURE FROM GOOLD BROWN

CLASSES OF THE LETTERS

The letters are divided into two general classes, *vowels* and *consonants*.

A *vowel* is a letter which forms a perfect sound when uttered alone: *a, e, o*.

A *consonant* is a letter which cannot be perfectly uttered till joined to a vowel: *b, c, d*.

The vowels are *a, e, i, o, u*, and sometimes *w* and *y*. All the other letters are consonants.

W or *y* is called a consonant when it precedes a vowel heard in the same syllable; as in *wine, twine, whine; ye, yet, youth*. In all other cases these letters are vowels; as in *newly, dewy, eyebrow*.

CLASSES OF CONSONANTS

The consonants are divided into *semivowels* and *mutes*.

A *semivowel* is a consonant that can be imperfectly sounded without a vowel, so that at the end of a syllable its sound may be protracted: *l, n, z*, in *al, an, az*.

A *mute* is a consonant which cannot be sounded at all without a vowel, and which at the end of a syllable suddenly stops the breath: *k, p, t*, in *ak, ap, at*.

The semivowels are *f, h, j, l, m, n, r, s, v, w, x, y, z,* and *c* and *g* soft. But *w* or *y* at the end of a syllable is a vowel. And the sound of *c, f, g, h, j, s,* or *x* can be protracted only as an *aspirate*, or strong breath.

Four of the semivowels—*l, m, n,* and *r*—are termed *liquids*, on account of the fluency of their sounds; and four others—*v, w, y,* and *z*—are likewise more vocal than the aspirates.

The mutes are eight: *b, d, k, p, q, t,* and *c* and *g* hard. Three of these—*k, q,* and *c* hard— sound exactly alike. *B, d,* and *g* hard stop the voice less suddenly than the rest.

PART 2A

For a great tutorial on the sounds of a famous poem, pick up Mary Oliver's book—very useful anyway for a young poet—and read her sound breakdown of Robert Frost's "Stopping by Woods on a Snowy Evening" (pp. 24–28).

In the meantime, let's do our own.

Read the following poem.

The Imprisoned Soul
Walt Whitman

At the last, tenderly,
From the walls of the powerful, fortress'd house,
From the clasp of the knitted locks—from the keep of the
well-closed doors,
Let me be wafted.

Let me glide noiselessly forth;
With the key of softness unlock the locks—with a whisper
Set open the doors, O soul!

Tenderly! be not impatient!
(Strong is your hold, O mortal flesh!
Strong is your hold, O love!)

I am not going to bother with a lot of terminology, because that isn't our focus here. I am going to talk about the sounds in general. But before I do, I'd like you to jot down what you thought about the sound of the poem. Answer these questions (feel free to go back over the poem, and even count if it helps). I supply my own answers further down, but please don't look at mine before having finished yours.

1. Which sounds (letters or pairs of letters) were the most dominant?
2. Did the poem sound soft or hard?
3. Did the sound of the poem agree with the subject of the poem?

My answers are upside-down on the next page.

PART 2B

Let's go back to that poem by Mary Oliver that ran at the beginning of the lesson. Can you answer the same questions you answered for Walt Whitman's without any help from me?

PART 2C

The final part of your assignment this week is to write a four-liner—just four lines— heavy on one or two particular sounds. Funny as it seems, tongue-twisters are great guides here (and a lesson in repetition as well):

> Peter Piper picked a peck of pickled peppers.
> A peck of pickled peppers Peter Piper picked.
> If Peter Piper picked a peck of pickled peppers,
> Where's the peck of pickled peppers Peter Piper picked?

You can find more here: uebersetzung.at/twister/en.htm

CHALLENGE EXERCISES

1. Read a paragraph of prose from your favorite book, examining it through the "Sound Microscope."

2. Read a poem in a foreign language that you don't know. Freed from distraction by meaning, you will focus only on the sound. With the sound rules from this week in mind, discuss with your mentor what feelings the poem's sound inspired.

3. Write a four-line poem that sounds "hard." Write a four-line poem that sounds "soft."

4. Come up with a word that illustrates each sound discussed by Goold Brown.

SOUND PERSONALITIES

Purpose: To develop personalities for words whose meanings we don't know.

In Week 5, I asked you to come up with personalities, using the 5 Senses, for abstract words whose meanings you knew. This week, as part of this unit on sound, we're going to do the same thing for words whose meanings you don't know. Doing an exercise like this helps us develop associations for words without being guided by their definitions.

For instance, take a word I read yesterday in a magazine: "prolegomena." I don't know what it means. Let's see how I do, using the 5 Senses:

- Prolegomena looks like … a mountain.
- Prolegomena smells like … lemon.
- Prolegomena feels like … sand.
- Prolegomena tastes like … a garden.
- Prolegomena sounds like … a rooster.

The best I can tell you is that the word sounded Greek to me (literally, not in the sense meant by the expression "it's all Greek to me"!) and, so, put me in mind of the countryside, monuments, fruits, vegetables—I guess because those are the things I think of when I think of Greece.

I can imagine other avenues for association: Something about the word feels mountainous to me—maybe simply because it's so long, massive, and monumental. Maybe I thought of the mountain—instead of a clock tower, or a skyscraper—only because I saw some mountains this week and they were fresh in my mind. Maybe it's because the tall "P" and the spire of the "l" made me think of tall things. Or maybe some of the component letters—l, e, o, m, n—came together in my mind as their own word—"lemon"—which explains how I ended up with the "smells like" comparison.

The good news is that there's no way to be wrong here. Whatever comes to mind for you is appropriate. The idea is to explore associations using something other than meaning. Some of the associations you come up with may be random; or they may come from trying to guess the meaning using clues other than the official definition. None of this is unacceptable; you're playing. Not every experiment yields a beautiful, ready-to-go poem. Sometimes, brain teasers like this one are simply a way of working out our language muscles, in this case the sound group.

PART 1

So, turn to the dictionary and find 10 words whose meanings you don't know. Cover up the definition side of the page so you don't get any hints. If you're stuck, here are some possibilities:

1. Rheumatism
2. Transcendental
3. Aborigine
4. Uxorious
5. Prevaricate

PART 2

Now come up with Five Senses personalities for each of the 10.

When you're done, it might be interesting to look up the actual meanings of the words. According to Merriam-Webster.com, "prolegomena" refers to "prefatory remarks" or an essay prefacing and explaining a longer work. That's all well and good—I probably could have guessed it if I'd paid close enough attention to the prefix's resemblance to the prefix in "prologue." But meaning was not my concern in this exercise. Still, I learned a new word. Okay, enough with this prolegomena—do the exercise.

CHALLENGE EXERCISE

An excellent way to practice seeding similar sounds throughout a poem is to find a long, unfamiliar word like "prolegomena" or "pulchritudinous" and to see how many other words you can make out of its component letters, just as in Scrabble. Then, after you've come up with at least a half-dozen, try to write several lines of poetry—at least four—which use all the words, the original and the six alternatives. Try to make as much sense with the mini-poem as you can. The purpose here is to scatter similar-sounding words so you can listen to their echo.

NONSENSE

STOP BEING SO RATIONAL!

Purpose: To record and write about dreams for a week.

Dreams have shaped art and literature for centuries. I don't mean only that writers have written about their dreams. I mean that writers have tried to make their poems *feel* like dreams—disconnected, surreal, illogical, but also magical in a way that "rational" poems are not. This week, we'll try to figure out how we might accomplish some of the same.

As you've surely experienced, dreams work according to a logic of their own. They have a logic, but it isn't the rational logic of our waking lives. Different situations become spliced together; characters wander from a setting in which you've experienced them to one in which you never have; you find yourself in places you have never been. **This week, you're going to try to capture that elusive logic by keeping a diary journal in which you're going to record every dream that you have** *immediately after you've had it.* So, every morning this week, as soon as you wake up—before you brush your teeth, before you put on your clothes, before you roll out of bed—immediately write down, as a series of bullet points or a narrative (as long or as short as you need), everything you remember about your dreams. It's okay if there's more than one; it's okay if you remember only fragments; just write down everything you remember, in as much detail as you can, as soon as you wake up. Keep your notebook dream diary right by your bedside, and in case you wake up in the middle of the night, write then, too, if there's something worth recording. As the saying goes, the best writer is the one who doesn't leave a good idea 'til the morning.

Once you're done, you will write a poem splicing together all the dream fragments you recorded. At first don't worry about line breaks, stanzas, and all the other good stuff particular to poetry. If it feels more manageable, you can start your assignment by writing a piece of prose connecting your dream fragments. After you're done, you can worry about how to make poetry out of it. (We'll talk more about this step below.)

What's the point of splicing together so many random images and feelings? To ramp up the randomness even more than a single dream does. What I'm trying to do is to get you to see poetry as a home for nonrational thought. This is a complicated concept that graduate students can study for five years, but it has meaning at your level, too. Poetry doesn't have to make the kind of sense that, for example, your essays do. You can think of poetry as a vacation from that kind of logic. This isn't to say that you can just throw down fifty random words and call it a poem. Poems *do* have logic—just not the logic of 2+2. In a poem, 2+2 can = 5. If this concept is a little strange for you, don't worry about it just now. Splicing together a bunch of dream fragments in a single poem is simply fun, leading to the same surprising turns of meaning as a good Mad Libs exercise.

But how to splice these dreams together?

A good way to get your notes started is to ask yourself questions related to the Five Senses:

- What did I see?
- What did I feel?
- What did I smell?
- What did I hear?
- What did I taste?

Your notes don't have to unfold in complete sentences. Just get the sensations down.

Let's say your notes about your dreams start off like this.

> **Monday:** Big, dark woods. There is some kind of ruined stone castle. Maybe I'm in England. I'm alone, I think. I keep looking for something, but what? Feeling anxious and a little scared. Not sure when it will end.

~

Tuesday: I'm trying to get to the back of the bus. It's yellow, like a school bus. It's not a long bus and there's no one in my way—not even sure there's anyone else on the bus—but I just can't make my way back there. It's like I'm walking through water, except even with water you move forward.

~

Wednesday: Kept seeing my friend Donnie, whom I haven't seen since I was a kid. He was all grown up, like an adult, even though we're the same age. But he had the same face as when I last saw him, when he was five.

~

Your spliced document doesn't have to incorporate the dreams in chronological order, and can mix and match the dreams at will:

Big, dark woods. I am alone, I think—and then there's Donnie, walking to the back of the schoolbus. It's just us two, and a couple of crows watching from the driver's seat. Donnie wants to know how old I am. Same as you, I tell him. I'm thirty-five now, Donnie says. What am I looking for in this castle?

I started with the first details of the first dream, and no sooner did I mention that I was alone than I remembered good ol' Donnie. Since I was leapfrogging dreams in this way, I thought I'd bring the schoolbus in from Tuesday. Which isn't very logical considering I'd just said I was in the woods. But that's the kind of thing that isn't going to trip us up in this exercise! Once I was moving along in this way, I decided it was perfectly fine to bring in some other elements that weren't necessarily part of the dreams: the crows driving the bus, for instance (another wonderful absurdity—how can crows drive a bus?!) And so on.

How might I render this prose segment into a poem? Well, I know I need lines and stanzas. I need to tighten up the language so that it reads like a poem instead of a story, and I could use some sharp images and description. I could spruce up the sound effects by thinking of letters/sounds that evoke the rustle of the woods (s, sh, w, zh, etc.—you might pick different ones) and the darkness (d, r, k—though maybe only because those are the consonants that make up the word "dark"). I'm not going to make a checklist of these things—just keep them in mind as I work:

> Big, dark woods.
> I am alone.
> Donnie walks toward me
> but he's not moving.
>
> The crows drive the schoolbus,
> yellow as a pony.
> They debate
> the news.
>
> The castle is nice,
> Donnie says.
> Though I am
> an old man.

≈

Do you see how the prose fragment transformed once again on its way into poetry? I decided to ramp up the illogic of the circumstances through Lines 3 and 4 of the first stanza: Donnie is walking without moving. (Huh? Exactly.) The crows are now driving the schoolbus, which is yellow, like a real schoolbus, but as "yellow as a pony," which makes no sense. Putting something not only real but very common, like a yellow schoolbus, in the same line as something absurd, like a yellow pony, is another powerful device in such nonsense poems. The careful insertion of something "real" into a completely fantastical setting always has a startling effect.

Anyway, I thought I'd make things even more zany by having my crows arguing about the news. And then Donnie says, "The castle is nice." What castle?! And what does his being an old man have to do with it?!

The poem makes no excuses for itself; that is, it doesn't explain why these unrelated impressions are all clumped together, how crows could be driving a bus, etc. It just tells this wacky story.

As for the craft aspects of the poem, my lines are pretty short. To me, that felt more tense than having long flowing lines—because the situation feels strange and tense.

So, what kind of feeling does this poem evoke in you? Perhaps it feels random and senseless, but surely it also evokes some feelings of unease, anxiety, disquiet, puzzlement, maybe even frustration? Those aren't feelings as easily evoked by a nice, logical poem. That was my point here. Poetry sometimes achieves its aims in some roundabout ways. Writing about dreams in a style that simulates the illogical flow of dreams is one way of achieving that.

Now it's your turn.

By the way, if there are elements of your dreams you'd like to keep private, feel free to. You don't have to share your notes—or, for that matter, the assignment—with the mentor.

If you're not much of a dreamer, see if someone you know—a sibling, a parent, a friend (people your age are best)—might serve as your guinea pig for the week and contribute their dreams. It's another kind of experiment entirely to work with the dreams of someone else. We are less possessive and defensive when we come to working with material from the lives of others; that is, we use it with much less self-consciousness, often leading to better results.

CHALLENGE EXERCISES

1. Prep by reading some poems about dreams (you can find a collection at famous-poetsandpoems.com/thematic_poems/dream_poems.html) and looking at the paintings of artists like Salvador Dalí, a surrealist who often painted visions from what can be called the dream life (just type "Salvador Dali images" into a search engine). Don't just look at Dalí's paintings. Think about what you're seeing: describe the painting to yourself in your notebook. Don't try to make sense of it; just capture it in words, as if you were describing something perfectly ordinary. For instance, about Dalí's famous *The Persistence of Memory* (be sure to look it up), you could note: "The pocket watch drips off a branch." That's a pretty good line for a poem, by the way.

2. Dreams are only one way of arriving at poetry that leaps around from image to image, sensation to sensation, without proceeding by the logic of prose. Often, poets will write about things without specifying for the reader what's under discussion, as a way of moving the poem away from questions like "What does it mean?" toward questions like "How does it feel?" or "What does it sound like?" A lot of poetry is frustrating because it's so hard to understand "what it means." But if you can free yourself from needing to understand what a poem means and enjoy it as a sound object, or a feeling object, you may help your enjoyment of poetry a great deal.

3. For an exercise, look up online the poem "The Hollow Men" by T. S. Eliot. Don't worry so much about what it means—though you can certainly look it up in an online encyclopedia. Just read it out loud—or have it read to you by the mentor—and listen, trying to pay attention to what the poem makes you feel.

ANTI-COMPARISONS

Purpose: To continue working outside meaning.

You've done comparisons. It's time for anti-comparisons. What are anti-comparisons? This is a made-up term. Comparisons seek out a shared quality between two things. For instance: "The sun is like an egg yolk." The sun and an egg yolk share a shape and a color. "The tree crown is a green cloud." The tree crown and a cloud don't share a color, but they do share a shape.

In anti-comparisons, the two compared things share nothing at all, at least not from a rational perspective. The desk is like a wood on fire. The pen is a tattered curtain. The coffee is like a slug after a rainstorm. These objects share nothing—not shape, not color, though in some cases they share a feeling of the kind I've been describing—less obvious than a meaning connection, but more mysterious and therefore potentially more enchanting. For instance, the association of pen and tattered curtain puts me in mind of a writer in a disheveled apartment, holding his pen in his hand and staring emptily at the tattered curtain in front of him as he tries to come up with an image or a word for his poem. There's something arresting about the image, as if that tattered curtain represents the writer's struggling mind.

You may be wondering why I would make you practice this stuff. This exercise aims to separate you even more from the idea that poetry has to make a conventional kind of sense. If you say to a neighbor "the coffee is like a slug after a rainstorm," that person is likely to look at you quizzically. If you say so in a poem, your reader—your best kind of reader—is going to perk up. Your reader isn't necessarily going to be able to say what this "means," but this won't ruin his experience of the poem. It'll simply create an experience different from the experience of a poem that's easily comprehensible.

So, this week, your job will be to come up with a dozen nonsense comparisons. However, please come up with three comparisons for each originating object/thing/feeling, etc. So, in all, you will end up with 36 comparisons. I am asking you to come up with three comparisons because I think your comparisons might only get weirder and better if you do more.

For instance, if my first coffee comparison is "like a slug after a rainstorm."

My second might be "like the trill of a telephone."

And my third might be "like playing in the mud."

I made an effort in each case, as you should, to think on the fly, to get an impression out before I could think about it too long. You'll notice that my second comparison is quite random, just like the first, but that the third circles back closer to coffee in its meaning. Coffee and mud aren't identical, of course, but they do share a dark color, they both have something to do with the earth, they both tend to be found in rural places. It's a different kind of comparison than something more standard, like "coffee beans are like peas" (shape) or "coffee is a dark sky" (color).

And, I would argue, it's more magical and surprising than if I hadn't done a couple of nonsense practice rounds first. That is, nonsense practice ultimately steers you back to sense (not a bad thing, as poems that are complete nonsense are quite tough to read) but a different kind of sense—the magical sense of poetry.

Your turn. **Come up with 12 objects/feelings/random words/what-have-you and find three comparisons for each.** Don't strain to make the third one in each case more "sensible." Just use your instinct and see what emerges. There's no way to be wrong here. If the third example is just as random as the first two, that's okay!

CHALLENGE EXERCISES

1. Come up with 10 anti-comparisons for a single object/thing/feeling, etc.

2. Write a poem about said object/thing/feeling, etc.

I'M A POET AND I DON'T KNOW [WHAT THE WORD MEANS]

Purpose: To conclude our nonsense practice by writing a poem full of words we don't know.

Remember "prolegomena"? It was the word I didn't know in Week 14. Usually, I'm not too happy when I run into a word I don't know—I wish I knew it!—but that week, it was a real help, because it got distracting old Meaning out of the way and helped me to focus on the sound and feeling of the word.

To further underscore this point, this week you are going to write a poem full of words you don't know. That's right: one per line! Let's say, for the sake of ease, the poem will consist of four stanzas of four lines apiece. It doesn't have to rhyme, but it can. Sixteen lines equals sixteen unfamiliar words. Any 16 words you don't know will do. You can find them randomly in the dictionary, or maybe you keep a list of words whose definitions you mean to look up some day. The only requirement is that they be words you don't know and can't guess the meaning of.

I'm going to open the dictionary and look around until I find 16 words I don't know (I'll be honest and not peek at their definitions. That would defeat the purpose, anyway.) I'll look up a healthy mix of nouns, verbs, and adjectives. (Insofar as I can tell what kind of word they are.)

PART 1

You do the same: **look for 16 unfamiliar words.**

Here I go:

1. topee
2. cuneate
3. bezel
4. fatidic
5. reticulate
6. quinsy
7. stipitate
8. pilei
9. argent
10. clavecin
11. zetz
12. pomander
13. tanager
14. xanthic
15. geminate
16. nankeen

Boy, the world is full of unknown words. And to write a poem using one per line! The only solution is to have fun.

PART 2

Your next step is to write a 16-line poem where every line features at least one of these words. (You can tweak the rules a little bit and use more than one in one line, and then zero in another.) How to begin? Find a word among your 16 that you can latch on to. For instance, below, I think I started with "quinsy" because it roughly reminded me of "question." Which, in turn, took me to "Answer me this…" You don't have to think past the first line at this point, because most likely the first line will suggest a broad direction for the second, and so forth, and you'll be surprised by the poem rolling along. And don't worry about craft concepts in this exercise, like whether you're using the most vivid comparisons or your lines end in interesting places. Just focus on not making sense. (If you complain about all the work in this textbook, just please tell me what class ever gives you instructions like that!)

Answer me this modest quinsy:
For you, pilei or pomander?
A mighty howl: Let pilei be for
Argent plebes.

So be it! I nominate nankeen instead.
A tanager of much renown,
A bezel even,
A topee master.

The Cuneate Council
Sits to geminate
On this clavecin
Like the Parliament of Zetz.

A xanthic session,
A fatidic debate!
And what will the mighty body stipitate?
The Head Judge reticulates: It's time for lunch!

～

I hope it won't surprise you to learn that I had no idea where the poem was going as I was writing it (and still don't quite know), except for the broad notion that someone is being asked to choose between two things, the decision then referred to some greater (and slightly ridiculous) body. But even this is too much detail to worry about. The meaning isn't the point here. The poem was a ton of fun to write. Its nonsensical nature was a liberation. I felt like I was working on a group of muscles I had never used before.

PART 3

Now, of course, for amusement's sake—and because this is a great opportunity to learn some vocabulary, which you should do as well after you've done your poem—I'm going to **look up definitions for the words and rewrite the poem replacing the Mysterious 16 with their definitions. This is the third part of your assignment; please do the same.**

1. topee—sun hat
2. cuneate—wedge-shaped
3. bezel—diagonal face at end of blade or chisel
4. fatidic—prophetic [could have guessed this one from the fat- prefix, which fatidic shares with fate, fateful, etc. This is good SAT prep, too!]
5. reticulate—to form into a network (v.), netlike (adj.)
6. quinsy—inflammation of the tonsils
7. stipitate—having or supported by a stalk
8. pilei—pl. of cap, as in mushroom
9. argent—silver or something silvery (n.)
10. clavecin—harpsichord
11. zetz—strike or hit
12. pomander—ball of potpourri, formerly carried on person to ward off disease
13. tanager— a kind of songbird
14. xanthic—yellow or yellowish
15. geminate—doubled, arranged in pairs
16. nankeen—firm, durable, yellow fabric

Some observations, having defined my words: Some of these might not go together too badly in a real poem! Xanthic and nankeen have a mutual interest; so do xanthic and argent, both being colors. I did, however, mistake certain sentence parts for others.

PART 4

In any case, **let's see what this poem looks like with the unknown words replaced by known ones** (with some minor adjustment). You do it, too. Feel free to turn adjectives into nouns, nouns into verbs, etc., if it helps the word fit.

> Answer me this modest inflammation:
> For you, mushroom caps or potpourri?
> A mighty howl: Let caps be for
> Silver plebes.
>
> So be it! I nominate cloth instead.
> A songbird of much renown,
> A chisel-blade even,
> A sun-hat master.

> The Wedge-shaped Council
> Sits in pairs
> On this harpsichord
> Like the Parliament of Strikes.
>
> A yellow session,
> A fateful debate!
> And what will this stalk-stocked body judge?
> The Head Judge nets the answer: Time for lunch!

Perhaps this new poem is an even finer bit of nonsense than the one with the Mysterious 16. Or maybe simply a different kind. Both have their pleasures, and neither is hampered by stodgy old Meaning. And now it's your turn.

CHALLENGE EXERCISE

Here's another way to observe the same effects (that is, using a trick to remove Meaning). Write down 10 words, whether you know them or not. Try to make them less everyday than "shirt" or "stove" and more specific than "history." Include a mix of nouns, verbs, adjectives—"cruise ship," "orangutang," "belch," "splotchy." Then pick 10 sentences randomly out of the newspaper, writing them out on a separate piece of paper, numbering them 1 through 10. In each, choose a word to scratch out. Then assign the list of 10 words you prepared numbers 1–10. And then drop those 10 words into the corresponding slots in the newspaper sentences. Some will surely just sound silly, but did you create any magical new combinations by accident?

WRITE A POEM

In keeping with our progress, there was a lot more poem-writing this year than last year. And you were introduced to more complicated craft skills and ideas, too. You've earned the right to write about whatever you wish—using whatever craft skills you'd like, or none at all. **Your only assignment this week is the same as last year's—write a poem.** What kind and how is up to you.

No challenge exercise this week.

MENTOR NOTES

PLOT

Here is a plausible map of the plot points, large and small, in "The Golden Goose."

1. Dullhead and his brothers go to the forest to chop wood.
   a. The first brother meets an old man who asks him to share his food, but he declines. He injures himself cutting the tree.
   b. The same thing happens with the second brother.
   c. Dullhead has been given poorer food, but he shares it with the old man. At the bottom of the tree he finds a golden goose.

2. The events at the inn where Dullhead goes to spend the night with his goose.
   a. One by one, the innkeeper's three daughters try to steal one of the goose's golden feathers and become stuck to the goose.

3. Dullhead's journey toward the town ruled by the king.
   a. A parson, a clerk, and two peasants all become stuck to the goose while trying to help pry the others off the goose.

4. The challenges assigned to Dullhead by the king.
   a. The king's daughter, who never laughed, laughs as soon as she sees Dullhead leading his procession.
   b. The king had promised his daughter's hand to whomever manages to make her laugh, but seeing Dullhead's simpleness, the king demurs and sets Dullhead a challenge.
   c. Dullhead has to find a man who can drink a cellarful of wine.
   d. Dullhead has to find a man who can eat a mountain of bread.
   e. Dullhead has to find a ship that can sail on both land and sea.
   f. Succeeding in all three, Dullhead finally claims the king's daughter as his bride.

How much detail is too much and how much isn't enough for this kind of outline? A good guideline, as mentioned above, would be: Can someone who hasn't read the story understand all its significant events by reading the outline alone?

~

As for the second part of the exercise, here were the moments when I found myself interested in the story and wanting to read on.

- As soon as we, the readers, learn that some character is treated badly by another (Paragraph 1), we develop a sense of pity for that character, and want to read on to see if he gets to triumph in some way. This gets at one of the essential qualities of plot: It benefits from **conflict**. Think about it. Think of two jockeys on horses, or two speed-skaters on a rink, even if you don't really care about horse-racing or ice-skating. Aren't you curious who's going to win? We human beings have a natural interest in competition and conflict. It's one of the things that makes us want to read on in a short story.

- Because Dullhead isn't like his oh-so-very-impressive brothers, we're curious to learn how he will do with the woodcutting task. The Grimms prolong the suspense by having his father say no, at first.

- I had a mild uptick of interest when the innkeeper's daughters tried to pry off the goose's feathers. Would they succeed? By this point, something should be becoming clear about this tale: It works in **sequences**. That is, part of its **structure**—each new "movement," as I've been calling it—includes a sequence of similar events (Dullhead and brothers cutting wood, innkeeper's daughters trying to pluck feathers, townspeople latching on to the girls, the king's challenges). Sequences are effective because they make us want to read on. We are naturally curious to get to the end of the sequence to find out whether its final element will differ or not. It does in the case of the brothers chopping wood and in the case of the king's challenges. It doesn't in the case of the innkeeper's daughters and the townspeople. This story keeps us guessing. **Frustration of the reader's expectations** is another smart plot tactic—but selectively, or the reader will get frustrated enough to put down the story!

- The next uptick of suspense is obvious: the king's challenges. Will Dullhead make it and get the hand of the king's daughter?

~

Finally, here are some potential answers to another question posed in the exercise: What else about the story either isn't plausible or is simply forgotten as a plot thread?

1. Where is Dullhead when the sisters are trying to pry off the goose's feathers? The story says he wasn't in the room when the first one tried, but it's hard to believe he didn't notice all night!

2. And whatever happened to the old man after he granted Dullhead's final wish? He disappears from the story!

SUSPENSE

Here are potential conflicts, climaxes, and resolutions for the situation ideas in the student section:

Situation: A remote farm has been enduring a record drought. If the rains don't come soon, the crop will wither, and with it, any chance of keeping the operation going. Out wandering one day, Riley, the youngest son, meets a Native American man who says he can direct him to a spring that holds enough water to irrigate the crops of 10 farms like his father's.

Conflict: Will the young man find water or come to harm?

Climax: The Native American does lead the young man to a spring. It runs past an impoverished Native American settlement.

Resolution: The young man brings water to his father's farm, but he's no longer interested in taking over his father's operation when he grows up. To his father's disappointment, he moves to the Native American settlement and becomes an advocate for improvements in their lives.

Situation: John is really short, but he's dying to make the basketball team.

Conflict: Will he make it?

Climax: During tryouts, John gets distracted by the team uniforms. They're pretty ugly and he has an idea for how to improve them. When his turn to shoot layups comes, he's busy drawing in a sketchpad in the corner.

Resolution: John doesn't make the team, but his career in graphic designer/advertising is launched.

~

Situation: Every time Mom plants flowers, a deer chews them up.

Conflict: Who will win this battle?

Climax: After months of losing, Mom holds a rifle out the bedroom window at 3:00 AM, waiting for the deer to show up.

Resolution: When he does, she can't pull the trigger. She concedes the battle. So her house won't have flowers.

~

By the way, notice that all these resolutions turn the stories away from the initial conflict. That is, they reveal a greater concern than will-he-or-won't-he? It's a sleight of hand, of sorts: The writer ropes in the reader by making him wonder whether Riley's father's farm will survive; whether John's going to make the team; whether the deer or Mom will win. But in each case that becomes too little to ultimately keep the reader's attention. In any simple conflict, the reader has a pretty good idea who's going to win—either one side or the other. So there isn't that much surprise if, indeed, in the outcome one of the two sides wins and that's all that happens. A one-side-versus-another conflict is enough to draw a reader in, but something more has to happen—some surprise, some unexpected revelation, a suggestion for a new way of seeing things—when the story ends. Look at your favorite short stories and you'll notice that the protagonists rarely get at the end what they were looking for at the beginning, even if they "win," or they rarely want the same thing if, indeed, it's theirs by the end of the story.

I confine this notion to the mentor guidance because it's too advanced for this lesson. But it would be useful for you, as the mentor, to absorb its logic so as to guide the student's practice of resolutions more knowledgeably.

STORY FROM A SENTENCE

Here are five sentences to follow starter sentence #1 in the student section, "The new family was different."

1. *The new family was different. You could hear their broken-down moving truck all the way up the lane. My great-grandfather planted the oaks that line the drive, so you could say their knocking one down on the way in didn't help things. My mother—it was her grandfather who planted the oaks—refused to go over with the pie she always baked for new neighbors. "I want to know how those raggedy people could afford one of these homes," she sniffed through the kitchen window, watching them unload their scuffed furniture. I waited until Mother went upstairs, then snuck over to the house next door.*

Different how? I asked myself as I tried to come up with a second sentence. I had no clues other than what was in that first sentence: The family was different. I decided to make the new family poor and the observing family wealthy. Not being wealthy myself, my instinct was to make the new family wealthy. As fiction writers, we tend to side with the downtrodden, writing from their perspective, but it's a great creative challenge to write from the perspective of someone unlike us. It exercises the imagination, not to mention empathy.

Okay, so they're poor. What would make readers understand that? How about their ramshackle moving truck? I saw it moving down a wide country lane. So in the second sentence I've given myself a moving truck and a lane. What might happen involving those two things? What if the truck mows into one of the trees that line the lane? And what if those trees were planted by the narrator's family? That wouldn't endear the new family, would it? The next sentence came easily: The mother is upset and refuses to be hospitable to the new neighbors. And that's when an interesting idea occurred to me, an idea ripe with the kind of conflict that moves a story forward: The mother may be furious at the new neighbors, but her child—we still don't know if it's a boy or a girl—is curious. S/he waits until Mother goes upstairs, and steals over to say hello to the neighbors.

Who are the new neighbors? How did they afford a home in such an expensive neighborhood? What happens when the narrator goes over? Does s/he make friends or enemies with the neighbors and their kids? If friends, does his/her mother find out? As you can see, these opening sentences leave a lot of tantalizing threads for development.

Below are some questions you can ask to prod the student if he's stuck coming up with ways to untangle the possibilities in the other four opening sentences:

2. *It's a well-known fact that thieves read the obituaries to know which houses will be empty during services for the deceased.*

   The writer has given himself lots here to keep himself busy for whole paragraphs. Who is the thief? Whose home is it? Who's died? Does the robber have a personal vendetta against these people? Or he doesn't know them?

3. *Molly and Tim loved one another more than anything else in the world, with the exception of their cats. So it was easy for them to join their lives, save for one thing: Their cats hated each other.*

   Another much-to-unspool setup. Did they try any methods to get their cats to like each other? Did they consult a vet? Did they take their cats to a cat psychologist? The first sentences of a story with this kind of opening sentence would probably be concerned with a (humorous) account of everything they had tried to make their cats get along.

4. *"Let a couple of pucks slide by you during the game," the man in the straw hat said to the goalie, "and there's a condo in Florida with your name on it."*

Here you have a sports scandal brewing. What kind of man is the goalie? Is he of questionable morals? Or is he squeaky clean? Or is he squeaky clean but he really needs some money urgently, and for a cause more noble than a condo in Florida? Where is this taking place? What's this team's record? What's the cost of losing this game for the team? Are they likely to win it otherwise? Do we know anything about the man making the offer?

5. *Kenny was older than us, and as sure as a bull, so whatever he told us to do, we listened. We should have known we would pay for it.*

This opening sentence sets up a little mystery. What happened that the narrator so regrets? We don't have to find out in the opening six sentences, or we could find out right away, and the mystery becomes: How did this come to pass?

WALKING BACKWARDS

Help the writer by asking her to imagine herself as a crack Hollywood screenwriter, called in at the last minute to save a script. The studio heads have decided to keep nothing from the first draft except the climax. Can the writer fill in and come up with a new story that ends in the same climax?

One way to brainstorm is to draw a line with a half-dozen or so way-stations. The 5th one should be labeled CLIMAX. The 6th one: RESOLUTION: The 1st can say SITU-ATION/QUEST, and #2–#4 can be CONFLICT. (Not all of these way stations have to be used in describing the conflict, but it often takes more than one entry to develop a conflict.)

So, what might deliver our hero to the climax in question? Try to think of books or movies where a similar climax has occurred. (Don't feel bad—screenwriters do this all the time. In fact, they live by it. "There are no new ideas," the American poet Audre Lorde has said. "Only new ways of making them felt.") By tweaking the premise, the writer can make a related situation/conflict her own. For instance, she can update the premise of "The Golden Goose" to modern times (as she'll have to for an assignment in several weeks).

Another way to come up with a situation that results in the climax is to ask the writer: Is the climax a positive development for the protagonist? A negative one? What would make it positive? What would make it negative? Which one is less important than the fact that doing this will force the writer to think about what kind of situation might make this a positive outcome, and what kind of situation might make it a negative one.

CHARACTER REFRESHER

Here's a list of the characters in the story:

1. Dullhead
2. Dullhead's parents
3. The "little old grey man" Dullhead encounters in the forest
4. The king's daughter
5. The king
6. The goose

Notice that characters don't have to be human. We'll learn about things like **anthropomorphization**—when nonliving things like the wind are given human characteristics such as anger or kindness—in a later lesson; for now, let's agree that the goose is very much a part of this story, even if she doesn't speak and does very little.

1. Dullhead is clearly meant to own our affections. His family looks down on him and the king distrusts him. Of course we want him to succeed! We root for him not least because other people abuse him—readers love siding with underdogs. It's a natural extension of human empathy. However, Dullhead is also kind, willing to share his humble meal with a man who needs it. So, he is both good and an underdog. He isn't especially smart or resourceful—he manages to satisfy the king's challenges thanks to his kindness to the old man, not because he's unusually talented—but that hardly makes us disapprove. All in all, Dullhead is the most likable person in the story, along with the old man.

To elicit some of these—or perhaps slightly different—impressions from the writer, ask questions like:

    a. Do you like Dullhead? Why or why not?
    b. Can you give me three adjectives that describe Dullhead?
    c. Is Dullhead mean?
    d. Is Dullhead smart?
    e. If Dullhead was arm wrestling with one of his brothers, who would you root for?

2. See below for a more detailed discussion of Dullhead's father, but I think we can agree that Dullhead's parents are meant to come off pretty badly here. They don't think very much of their son, and treat him less kindly than they do his brothers. This opinion, shaped early on, doesn't change for us throughout the story, in part because the family members never come up again. (A fairy tale of this sort often has a variation, whereby the previously mean family learns that the previously disdained child has had success, and suddenly shows up, sweet as honey, wanting to share in the spoils. The story of Cinderella and the Biblical story of Joseph and his brothers are variations on this format. In both cases, the previously cruel family members repent for their ill treatment of the protagonist.)

Questions to ask the writer:

    a. Do you think Dullhead's parents love him?
    b. Do they treat him fairly?
    c. If you were a parent of Dullhead's, how would you act if he asked you to go chop wood in the forest?
    d. What do you think Dullhead thinks about them?

3. The "little old grey man" is quite a mystery, isn't he? Is he a human being or not? We don't know. Do we have to? Probably not. Not knowing that takes nothing away from our comprehension of the story. (I don't know about you, but I did find myself wondering whether Dullhead wasn't getting an awful lot in return for simply sharing some food with the man. Not only did he get the goose, but he also got three wishes to satisfy the challenges posed by the king. Not a bad deal!) In any case, to tally up: The little old grey man was both kind (his generosity to Dullhead) and severe (his punishment of the brothers). That

made him an interesting character for me, a combination of both traditionally positive (kindness) and less-than-positive (severity and punishment) qualities. It was hard to judge him, conclusively, though, because he never came up again.

Questions for the writer:

    a. Do you like the old man? Why or why not?
    b. Did the old man help anyone? Did he hurt anyone?
    c. The people he hurt, did they deserve to be hurt?
    d. The people he helped, did they deserve to be helped?

4. Now, the king's daughter is a genuine mystery. What had prevented this person from laughing ever before? Was it because she was a studious and scholarly girl? Was it because some tragedy had befallen her, perhaps having to do with her mother, who doesn't seem to be in the picture? We don't know. And to be honest, even though the king's daughter is a secondary character, I wouldn't mind knowing. This kind of background for a character is known as **backstory**. It isn't essential for every character we encounter—just think of the old man in the forest; we don't care whether he's human or not, where he comes from, or what *his* motivations are. But I did find myself wondering, in the king's daughter's case. It's hard to read something like "Jim refused to eat strawberries" without wondering why. The authors piqued my curiosity and never satisfied it.

    a. How do you feel about the king's daughter?
    b. Do you think she's beautiful?
    c. If you had to come up with a reason why she hasn't laughed in a long time, what would it be?
    d. If you had to try to make her laugh, how would you do it?
    e. After all this, what do you think of her?

5. The king wasn't too kind to Dullhead. Instead of judging Dullhead for himself, he believed rumors that said Dullhead wasn't very impressive. But he didn't push Dullhead away for good. He set him all sorts of challenges. But when you think about it, weren't those challenges a little bit strange if the king's aim was to make sure his daughter would be treated well by this person? On the other hand, anyone who can find men to drink a cellarful of wine and eat a mountain of bread, as well as procure a ship for both land and sea, is someone who's probably

resourceful enough to take care of somebody's daughter. So, all in all, the king's challenges may have been reasonable. In short, the king isn't especially lovable, but we don't dislike him as much as we do Dullhead's parents. What do you think?

    a. Summarize the king's actions throughout the story.
    b. Do you think the authors meant to make him a likable character?
    c. What's one plot detail that would have made him a more likable character?
    d. What's one plot detail that might have made him a less likable character?

6. The goose is a bit of a mystery, too. Is he alive or not? We don't know. The goose never speaks, never does anything, in fact, unless you consider his stickiness a part of his character. The goose is what's known as a **passive** character. Everything happens to him; he takes no action and expresses no desire of his own.

    a. How do you feel about the goose?
    b. Do you think the goose and the old man know each other?
    c. Do you think the goose likes Dullhead?
    d. What do you think is going through the goose's mind at various points in the story? Is he laughing at Dullhead? Rooting for Dullhead? Wishing another of the brothers found him? Invent, if you'd like.
    e. After all this, what do you think about the goose?

One thing worth pointing out is that the tale leaves as much left out when it comes to character as it did in plot, as we discussed last week. For instance, we never do learn whether Dullhead is actually secretly intelligent, and simply nobody knew, or that he isn't very smart after all, but only kind. If you think about it, these would make for very different takeaways from the story. If Dullhead was secretly intelligent, we would walk away from the story feeling like his parents were mean and inattentive. But if he wasn't, if he was merely kind? Nothing justifies meanness, but maybe his father wasn't so cold-hearted when he was trying to prevent Dullhead from going to the forest? Maybe he was thinking of his son's safety? I am stretching the facts a little bit to make that last point—Dullhead's father is a pretty mean man. Even if he was thinking only of his son's safety, there was no need to say so by referring to the fact that Dullhead's brothers were more intelligent. But every little detail adds to our notion of a character's qualities, and the absence of that information often leaves us uncertain. (These nuances will come into play more in Week 7, when the writer will have to come up with a more complicated character.) That may not be such a bad thing. If we were uncertain about the main character—and we are, to some degree—it's a bigger issue than if we were uncertain about a minor one, like Dullhead's father. And even though the story never clarifies whether Dullhead is both intelligent and kind or merely kind, that appears to be beside the point for the author. The story's point seems to be that goodness has to do not only with how smart or accomplished someone is, but what's in his heart.

A CHARACTER WITH WANTS

Help the student come up with characters on a quest by practicing with favorite books, stories, or even some newspaper articles in the local paper. Even a seemingly bland story about a town council meeting regarding a proposed bike lane on the local highway is full of characters on a quest: One side, presumably, wants the lane; the other does not. In fact, you could probably look around yourself and note half a dozen objects that remind you of quests and obstacles. The stove may remind you that your daughter is on a quest to lose 10 pounds by next month, or that your son is on a quest to put on 10 pounds because he wants to become a wrestler. The fields in the distance may remind you of the iffy weather that has threatened crops for local growers, many of whom are hanging on by a thin thread. The basketball hoop may remind you of the local school's basketball team, which will be cut for budget reasons if it doesn't achieve a better-than-even record this year, which would be a first for the team in a decade.

Getting the writer to notice the ubiquity of quests and obstacles should ease him into the task of coming up with 10 situations of his own. In each case, the prompting questions are:

- Who's the character?
- What does he want?
- What's standing in his way?
- What are we curious to find out?

LET'S FACE IT, WE'RE COMPLICATED

The guidance is plentiful in the lesson itself, but a note about complicated characters. Complicated characters are, well, a complicated issue for mentors working with young writers. Fiction doesn't work when the goal is to try to write nice stories about nice people. That simply isn't what people in real life are like, or, if they are, those aren't the ideal characters in fiction because they aren't very compelling. This is, understandably, tricky terrain for, say, parents trying to raise conscientious, moral young men and women. But chronicling human imperfection in art by no means requires depravity in life. As the great French novelist Gustave Flaubert said, "Be a bourgeois in your life and a madman in your art." That is, what goes in one need not affect the other. There are plenty of alcoholic poets and those mythologized writers who went mad from the demands of their craft, but neither of these are requirements of the job. The only requirement is: Show the world as it really is. And it's really complex.

However, the young writer may be self-conscious about showing you just how morally complex he's capable of being. He may be invested in impressing you as a good kid. So supervise lightly this week. Don't ask to see all the writer's work. Ask to see only that which he might like help with. And try to make him feel like the shaky moral terrain in which he's observing his character is a perfectly legitimate place to explore. Reassure him that it need not reflect on who he is in "real life."

LISTENING TO YOURSELF TALK

Dialogue takes longer to figure out than other aspects of craft. That's because a writer's first instinct is to forget how "ungrammatical" and casual spoken speech is. There's something about the computer screen or legal pad that makes us tense up and get formal. It's understandable—spoken speech vanishes into thin air. Written speech sticks around, so we feel obligated to get it right.

A writer of dialogue in fiction has to get over all that. The most useful thing you can do for the writer in this lesson is point out all the instances of informal and ungrammatical speech in the recording: the swallowed sounds and words, the misspoken words, the indirect responses, and so on. You can also preview our dialect lesson later in this series by sensitizing the writer to how differently people in different places (and of different cultures) pronounce the same things.

I understand that this lesson works against, to some degree, something else you're trying to do for the writer: help him become an accurate speller, a knowledgeable user of grammar, etc. But just as the depiction of morally complex characters in art need not lead to transgression in one's own life, writing incorrect speech does not need to result in an impoverishment of the writer's own. The key thing is to contextualize the activity properly for the writer. That's where you come in. There's plenty of narrowly practical guidance in the lesson itself. What only the mentor can do is reaffirm the philosophy here: Rendering characters who have inaccurate speech makes them more lifelike, and the job of fiction is representation, not idealization. By the same token, inaccurate speech is for the page and the page alone. Good spelling and grammar remain noble and valuable goals, outside of fictional dialogue.

GOING FURTHER WITH DIALOGUE

We haven't talked about revision yet, but dialogue is one of those craft elements that, in my experience, benefits especially from several drafts. Counterintuitively, it's so hard to get the sound of speech just right. Maybe that's because we're listening to it in our minds, and the mental "listen" function works less well than the mental "imagine" function. So you may wish to counsel the writer to rewrite the lines once, spend a day or two paying extra attention to how people speak, and then try those lines again. Paying special attention to how people speak in those intervening days may sensitize the student to dialogue and give her ideas on how to fine-tune the update of the fairy tale.

As mentioned in the lesson, reimagining the dialogue becomes much easier when the direction is concrete ("Imagine Dullhead as Dustin, a young man who wants to attend college, though his parents don't think him up to it") than abstract ("render this as modern dialogue"). Whether you settle on my concrete example or choose one of your own, it may help the student to jot down as many notes as practical about the new plot, setting, etc. All of it will provide ideas for dialogue.

On the next page is my stab at some of the lines in the story.

Original Version	Revised Version

"If I give you my cake and wine I shall have none left for myself; you just go your own way."

"I don't have a lot for myself. Be on your way, alright?"

"Whatever I give to you I deprive myself of. Just go your own way, will you?"

"Whatever's yours ain't mine. Keep on your way."

So then Dullhead said: *"Father, let me go out and cut wood."*

"Dad, I want to try it. Please?"

But his father answered: *"Both your brothers have injured themselves. You had better leave it alone; you know nothing about it."*

"Quit nagging me. If it was too much for your brothers, likely it'll kill you. Leave it alone."

But Dullhead begged so hard to be allowed to go that at last his father said: *"Very well, then—go. Perhaps when you have hurt yourself, you may learn to know better."*

"Fine. You need to feel it on your own hide, I see. My granddad said once, 'The only mistakes you learn from are the ones that you make.' Go, go. You'll hurt yourself, and then you'll know."

Note that it's perfectly acceptable for the writer to introduce new plot elements into the quotes, such as "My granddad said once, 'The only mistakes you learn from are the ones that you make'."

DIALOGUE AS PLOT

Help the writer by brainstorming together both the situation and the characters. Ask about natural pairings—that is, situations when it would be natural for two people to be speaking. How about the writer and a sibling? That's a good one, not least because the writer is already familiar with her relationship with the sibling and can bring it onto the page. If the writer plays sports, a conversation between her and a coach or a teammate would work. If she collects stamps, a conversation between her and another member of the philately club where she sends away for stamps could be interesting.

In fact, if the writer is struggling to come up with a situation, characters, and dialogue, you can direct her to some previously written scene. A great modified version of this exercise is to take an already-written scene and figure out ways to adjust the dialogue so all the information outside of it can get packed into it. This is doable with a published story as well. Ask the writer to pick a favorite, and do the same thing.

It might also help to read some fantastic dialogue together. In my mind, the modern master of dialogue in fiction is Tobias Wolff. Pick up an old collection like *In the Garden of the North American Martyrs*, or his recent collection of new and selected short stories, *Our Story Begins*.

You might also help the writer by role-playing as the second speaker, so that he can hear the words spoken out loud, and have to figure out the speech and motivations of only one of the characters.

SETTING

Help the writer by brainstorming potential resettings for the story. If the writer moves it to a factory, how could he animate the main themes—an underdog, a desired outcome, a set of challenges, etc? Perhaps Dullhead is a welder who wants the chance to work on a new project, and Dullhead's parents, in this version, are replaced by the boss who won't take a chance on him and sets him a series of challenges so he can prove he's up to the task? (In this scenario, the character of the boss conflates both the parents and the king, which is fine. Replicating every single aspect of the tale exactly isn't the primary goal here.)

If the writer decides to move the setting closer to her own life—say, the town where she lives, and perhaps the tennis team that she plays for—Dullhead can become Derrick, a younger player who's promising but too young to compete in the upcoming county-wide championship, according to the coach. He begs the coach to give him a shot, and the coach says that a spot is his if he can beat the senior-most players on the team.

I think you can see where I'm going with this. Almost every setting incorporates the possibility of investigating the themes explored by the Grimms in the tale. And this one gives the sports buffs a chance to practice their knowledge.

USING SETTING TO CREATE A MOOD IN A SHORT STORY

If the student is stuck, here are some examples of places that could conjure the emotions above, plus some trigger words that might make it easier for the student to imagine such a scene.

1. A feeling of depression, a sense of a place being down on its luck (downtrodden, sad, helpless)
   - A windswept street with many boarded-up windows and few pedestrians
   - An old kitchen with peeling linoleum, cheap wooden wall paneling, and low ceilings

2. A sense of terror (fear, goosebumps, a scream)
   - The scene inside a plane as it tumbles out of the sky
   - A dark alleyway

3. A sense of anxiety and uncertainty (uneasy, nervous, irritable)
   - A schoolroom where 30 high-school seniors will take their SATs
   - A schoolroom where 30 new American citizens will pledge allegiance to their adopted country

4. A sense of triumph, success, confidence (enthusiasm, smile, pride)
    - A flower shop
    - The dais where university graduates receive their diplomas from the Dean

BASIC POINT OF VIEW

This lesson refreshes—and deepens—the writer's recollection of the difference between first-person and third-person telling. In this exercise, I ask the writer to think about the implications of each for the kind of information that gets revealed in a story and how it's revealed.

As the writer retells a portion of the tale from the perspective of one of the characters, prompt him by asking: What does this character care about? What is he likely to focus on? What are his daily concerns? What is he likely to want to talk about, if he's getting to tell the story to an audience? The concerns of a story shift depending on who's telling it. The goose has to get around to telling the story of Dullhead and the king's daughter, but he's going to tell it from a very different set of concerns and observations than somebody else. This exercise is meant to emphasize that.

One good way to brainstorm would be to draw several columns across the top of a notebook page: for instance, Dullhead, goose, king, king's daughter.

Down the left-hand margin of the page, write several questions:

1. Three words to describe the character
2. First thing s/he does in the morning
3. The biggest problem in his/her day
4. Where does s/he live?
5. What does s/he want?

Then have the writer answer each question briefly for each of the characters, inventing the answer if she has to. These answers are likely to provide good material for the retelling from that person's perspective. (In addition to practicing character development!)

One note: Retelling the story from the perspective of the king or the king's daughter presents a challenge because they're not around for the first part of the story, so they have no way of knowing what happened then. But they have no way of knowing only in the current version of the tale. In the writer's version, they might know because Dullhead told them, or because the king happened to be eavesdropping on a conversation between Dullhead and the king's daughter, or vice versa. The writer doesn't have to be limited strictly to what happens in the story.

FIRST-PERSON VS. THIRD-PERSON NARRATION

Having discussed, last week, the difference between first-person and third-person narration and the way factors like motive and mood affect point of view, we're ready to dig deeper.

Once the writer has settled on a situation—some more potential situations follow—work with him to choose a character for first-person narration. Perhaps it would be easier if the character was similar to the writer, so he can feel familiar with the character's thoughts. Ask the writer what the character might be thinking about in the situation at hand. What's his mood? (If he's returning from work, maybe he's tired but happy.) Where does his mind wander while he's there? (That is, what's worrying him?) What is the first thing he has to or will do as soon as the situation at hand is over? What was he doing before he showed up in the situation? How does he feel about the other people present?

Once the student is ready to write, the answers to these questions can populate the 250-word segment. Since the segment is conveying the internal thoughts of a character, there will be a lot of "he thought" or " he wondered" or "he decided," as in "He would be pretty happy to get home as soon as possible, he thought."

Emphasize to the student all the ways in which a first-person narrator has no access to what's going on in the minds of those around him. Ask: What does the narrator think about Person X? What does he think Person X is thinking right now? Is he right? Does his mistaken idea of what Person X is thinking lead him to take any action? For instance, if the first-person narrator thinks Person X is ignoring him, he might say something nasty and walk out of the room. But a third-person omniscient narrator would know that Person X is merely shy.

Speaking of third-person narration, stress to the writer the ways in which this narrator knows everything about what everyone's thinking. He can tell the reader who's thinking what, who's right and who's wrong in his perceptions of others, and so on. The segment should reflect this understanding.

Some more ideas for situations:

- A family gathered around the dinner table.
- Three generations of a family—grandmother, mother, daughter/granddaughter—at a family picnic.
- Church congregation on a Sunday morning.
- Football team at practice.
- An orchestra in rehearsal for a big performance.

WRITING A SCENE FROM SCRATCH

Some writers will prefer starting to write the scene and developing the plot, characters, etc. as they go. Others will want to plan ahead. For the planners, it may be helpful to start with plot or character. The writer can push off those to fill in the other categories. An idea for situation or plot (which follows the basic guidance of the plot lessons, that is, features suspense) like "man grabs wrong suitcase from airport carousel" already has a built-in character (the man), and a setting (airport, and more broadly, either a city he's visiting or the home he's returning to, both of which raise questions the author can answer, filling his story with more detail). That would have been tougher to come up with if the writer had started with "airport" or "man at airport." However, a character with a quest, like "Johnny wants to beat the world record for the fastest mile" is also promising. It has a built-in plot, though no setting or point of view. A situation involving plot and character is the most promising departure point for a story; "story from dog's point of view" is a cool idea, but it still needs a situation. "Story from point of view of dog chasing Johnny, who has strapped beef steaks to a belt to set the dog in pursuit and make himself run faster"—that's more promising.

Once the writer has a situation, he might brainstorm about the other ingredients. Where is this taking place? Will he describe it directly or between the lines? If directly, the writer may wish to jot some notes in order to have ready material when he's writing. From whose point of view? The writer might think about whether to have the man at the airport narrating his own story versus a disembodied third-person narrator, and what that would mean for the narrative. It depends on the plot. If the story becomes about the men chasing him—because he has unknowingly picked up a suitcase full of uranium—probably a first-person narration would be tough to pull off, because we would be trapped inside the man's mind, and presumably he has no idea he's being followed. Dialogue is also possible to practice outside the scene, but I find dialogue to benefit most from creation right in the moment, as the scene is proceeding and the writer is "listening" to the characters in his mind. It's more immediate, which helps the dialogue, and it's especially hard to predict before starting what kind of dialogue will prove best.

PLAYING WITH THE VARIABLES IN A SCENE

If the writer is stuck, start by having her rearticulate the basics of the original. For instance, what's the plot? Ask the writer to write it down in one or two sentences. Then have her underline key details in these sentences, making sure that she ends up with at least half a dozen. Then ask her to come up with substitute details. So, instead of a funeral, let's say it's a visit by the president. Or a fair day. Or a car race. Tell the writer not to worry about whether she'll manage to make the story's theme (brothers, competition, etc.) work with the new situation. She will. Practically all themes are universal.

As the writer returns to the actual narrative, substituting the new plot reality for the old one, ask her to discuss with you out loud all the consequences of the plot shift for other elements of the story. For instance, if the new plot has to do with a celebratory fair, the author can't have black Town Cars inching to the cemetery and everyone talking about a death. The content of the story changes, the setting changes, the mood changes, the dialogue changes—everything. That's the idea here: to sensitize the writer to how interrelated the moving parts of this machine are. You can't shift one without having to rebuild the whole house of cards. This is part of why writing a story is so hard—an author has to be thinking along multiple lines at once—and why revision is so critical (something we'll focus on more in coming levels). Even a genius can't do a bang-up job in so many departments on the first try.

ANOTHER SCENE FOR THE SAME STORY

Refer to mentor guidance in Weeks 15 and 16.

WRITE A SHORT STORY

Let the writer know that you're available for discussion or brainstorming as she needs. But let her be in the driver's seat this week, writing without the expectation of supervision. Do make sure she has done the assignment, and do invite her to discuss her experience with you afterward—for instance, whether it was liberating, or frightening, to write without active mentoring. But try your best to let the writer drive the discussion, and if there's nothing she wishes to discuss, so be it.

WHAT DO POETS WRITE ABOUT?

It's not very easy to instruct a writer "how to write about _____"; such a lesson can offer only a sprinkling of examples. Broaden its impact by exploring other examples of writing via the Internet, the library, perhaps a local college whose poetry instructors would be willing to advise. (They would probably make a great resource in lots of other ways. Poetry departments are not used to being flooded with requests of interest from high-school-level students.)

This lesson implies that subject matter is what brings a poet to a poem. Not necessarily; or, rather, it isn't broad subjects that do it, for the same reason abstractions don't work well in fiction or poetry. A poet doesn't generally set out to write a poem about love or family; more often, he notices something, like that he is finally taller than his father, and writes a poem about that. Make sure to convey this to the writer. In a couple of weeks, we will practice it.

Note as well that poets hardly focus on the grandiose. They find the universal through the limited and specific. The owl inTennyson's poem becomes a commentary on animal nature in arguably a far more powerful way than D. H. Lawrence's head-on analysis of the matter in "Piccadilly Circus." Same goes for the Walt Whitman poem. And the fact that he chose to make it 3 lines instead of 30 makes those three lines ring that much louder. They may be about nothing much, but that nothing much sings loud because of how little of it there is. It was a courageous move to write only three lines.

You should draw the poet's attention as well to the fact that not all of the poems above succeed every step of the way. Overly perfect rhyme sounds false in our day, and, as discussed above, I think Tennyson's poem is better than Lawrence's, though "better" is relative. Perhaps it would be wiser to say that they handle the same subject in different ways, and Tennyson's affected me more. You and the poet might have different reactions.

In a poem like "Mending Wall," ask the writer to rewrite it as a piece of prose and chop it up in a new way. This should offer a window into why Robert Frost broke up the poem the way he did—or not. Ultimately, often we can only guess as to why a poet made the choices that he did. The asking and wondering why is the enjoyment of the poetry—not always the securing of a certain answer.

Poetry is a fusion of subject and style/craft. This week focuses on the former, but as you can see, there is no way to disentangle them. A three-line poem about a sinking ship or love for a dying elder or a hummingbird will ring differently than one about a farm. That depends on what's happening on the sinking ship or with the hummingbird, but just as much on what kind of sound the lines have, what form, and so on.

FINDING MAGIC IN THE ORDINARY

Some other ordinary things that could form the basis for a great poem:

1. Mom and Dad speaking to each other in the kitchen
2. Family breakfast
3. What you see out the nearest window
4. An argument with your siblings
5. The plants in the house
6. You're hungry
7. Collecting the leaves in autumn
8. Shoveling snow in winter
9. Waves crashing onto the shore
10. Chefs cooking in an open kitchen

It's very difficult to teach poetry because so much of it depends on a spark that lights up for different reasons in every poem. Often, it happens during the process of writing the poem, not through preplanning, though in my preplanning, I managed to come up with a pretty cool image, namely the traces of previous meals on Mom's apron, that took me far in the poem itself.

The 10-liner in this exercise isn't meant to form a complete poem. It can break off at 10 lines. (I continued because I was eager to finish my thought, as the writer may be, too.) It was satisfying for me to try my hand at the poem after thinking about it for so many steps, but I couldn't have written that poem without those steps. Help the writer brainstorm by asking questions like:

- What did you see?
- How did it make you feel?
- Did you notice something that surprised you? Made you feel sad? Worried? (Our best poems are about the things about which we feel strongly.)
- Who do you wish saw the things that you saw alongside you?
- Did you learn anything?
- Did it change your mind about anything?

Here are some ways to describe the sample "ordinary things" proposed in the lesson.

1. It all depends on how Mom and Dad communicate. The mother and father of a friend of mine come from different cultures: she from Brazil, where people stand very closely when speaking to each other, he from England, where personal distance is more customary. So whenever they speak to each other, she's walking toward him, and he's backing up. This could be fun to describe as the interaction of two armies.

2. The family at breakfast could be described as an animal family at breakfast, in the animal's natural habitat, wherever that is.

3. The field out the nearest window could be the beard of a giant face, the face being Earth itself. This could lead to a poem about Earth as the biggest face in the world, and all the things in the world—bridges, skyscrapers, fields—as various facial features.

4. This also depends on the participants' communication style.

5. The plants in the house could be trees in a colony on another planet where everything gets compressed and miniaturized. So, your home is the whole of the colony then. (And you and your family are space pioneers.)

6. I experience hunger as a giant emptiness of some kind. A poem about it could describe the hungry person as an empty drum, banging out a song of longing (for mashed potatoes, if you want to add a touch of humor.)

7. Collecting the leaves in autumn = shaving the earth-beard.

8. Shoveling snow in winter = a baker harvesting flour for the biggest cake in the world.

9. Waves crashing onto the shore have the regularity of other natural phenomena, such as low and high tide, sunrise and sunset, and could be described as a mundane member of nature's workforce, doing the same job every day, rotating shifts, dealing with the boss ... Waves lapping the shore also look like lots of things, such as a tongue spitting out water, or the ruffles at the edge of a skirt.

10. Chefs cooking in an open kitchen look like white ants wrestling with fire.

WRITING POETRY ABOUT THE EXTRAORDINARY

There's a difference between finding the extraordinary in the ordinary (last week's concern) and something extraordinary. The distinction is probably a little too subtle and abstract for the writer at this point, but you should try to understand it. In the first case, the imagination has to take the vision in question from the ordinary to the extraordinary. An aerial photograph of San Francisco's bays, bridges, and tunnels swathed in fog depicts something ordinary. But a mind that can then transform this vision of an American city into a vision of some spectral, futuristic planet swimming in vapor has created something extraordinary out of it. Meanwhile, if something out of the ordinary was going on in San Francisco—extraterrestrials had landed, or, more simply, there hadn't been a day of fog in a whole year—that's unusual and probably extraordinary (to San Franciscans, at least!).

How does a subject like this become a poem? Not very differently from the brainstorming process described in the opening weeks. An idea for a poem becomes a poem through the application of craft. Craft will be our focus later in this level. For now, we're focusing on the starting point of most poems: What to write about?

If the writer is struggling to come up with real or invented extraordinary sightings, ask her about the last nonrealistic movie she saw—perhaps *Harry Potter* or *The Lord of the Rings*? She can import a character or event or object or experience from that film into our world. What about the real and extraordinary? That's where observation comes in.

Drive together to a little-visited spot in your town, like a creek or a power plant or a bird-watching spot. Observe together. You are bound to notice something unfamiliar pretty quickly.

As for what about the experience to focus on, ask the writer to speak out loud some feelings and impressions about the sighting. A poem can simply describe what the writer is seeing, but it might become stronger if she brings herself—her opinions about what she's seeing—into it. It's difficult to guide exactly what a poem should focus on because it depends so heavily, as above, on the poet's own idiosyncratic thoughts and reflections. Use my experience as a guide.

The starting point, as in Week 2, is notes: If you're in a bird-watching spot and you notice something unusual—say, two birds fighting in the air—ask the writer to record as much as she can about what she's seeing, what it makes her think of, what feelings it evokes.

Then ask her to choose several images from her notes and find comparisons for them.

Then ask her to write out several impressions as sentences. Read the sentences out loud to her several times. Ask her whether, in listening to you, she sensed natural places to break the lines if they were to become part of a poem.

The focus of this first section is what to write about. Because one can hardly decide what to write about without delving at least a little into how to write about it, these early lessons also supply a little crash course in craft. Its basics—lines, stanzas, rhythm, description, etc.—will be our focus much more squarely in the rest of this year's practice.

FROM THEMES TO SITUATIONS

If the writer is struggling to find a concrete situation that illustrates the abstraction, set the exercise aside and do an association exercise: Which five or 10 concrete words does "gratitude" bring to mind? The writer might say "cookies" or "snow day." In turn, cookies might remind him of his last visit to Grandmother's, whereas "snow day" will remind him of school.

Conversely, when the student needs to come up with the abstraction himself, play a game of: Let's name the first 10 things we see. (Microwave, grass, pen, table, sun, etc.) You'll notice, by the way, that all these items are fairly concrete. It's a wonderful example of the way the human brain works. The human brain rarely thinks: "Ah, integrity." Rather, it thinks: "Guy cheating." But you can "rewind" these concrete items back into abstractions: electricity, writing, wood, warmth, etc. And—*voila!*—you already have your concrete answers for them.

However, you may wish to up the ante and ask the writer to come up with specific situations involving these concrete objects:

1. Microwave—An old man warming his TV dinner
2. Grass—Dad mowing it
3. Pen—A deliveryman in crisp white pants and shirt, a dull black stain under the shirt pocket where a pen exploded
4. Table—A game of cards, where the wager is a man's freedom (speaking of abstractions, that's one)

5. Sun—A man wandering through the Moroccan desert, with nary a drop to drink … (Come to think of it, this is more apt for a thriller film than a poem. By virtue of already having appeared in so many films and such, the proverbial man wandering in a desert has become an abstraction of his own.)

As for the mini-poem in the challenge exercise, the same logic as last week applies: Technical matters like number of lines are less important than close, vivid description and deployment of that "special eye" that's going to vacuum up all the unusual details of the moment.

You may wish to illustrate to the writer how much more difficult it is to write poems about abstractions than concrete situations. Ask: Can you write a poem about loneliness? How about an old man warming his TV dinner by himself? The latter will set the writer's mind aflame with far more ideas than the former.

To help him in the writing, prompt the writer by asking questions about the situation: Why is the man by himself? What is he eating? Is he actually watching TV, or reading? If so, what is he reading or watching? What does his home look like? Where is it located? What does the street look like? What is he wearing? How is his home decorated? Did he work that day or is he retired? And so on. A poem—like a story—doesn't have to (shouldn't, in fact) incorporate all this information. But rehearsing some of it may set the writer's pen moving. A single direction like this is more than enough to explore in a single poem.

EVERY WORD HAS FIVE SENSES

The writer is likely to have a hard time getting started—that is, thinking of emotional associations for the abstraction. (By the way, a fun alternative to the writer's having to come up with abstractions in the first place is to have family members come up with them and throw them into a hat, from which the writer could choose.) After the writer has five abstractions, call them out—"destruction," "bright," "create"—and ask the writer to jot down the first associations that come to mind. Use the word version of the Rorschach blot game that psychologists use: Ask the writer to say the first thing that comes to mind when the writer hears the word. It doesn't have to be logical. Then the writer can divide these associations up by the senses.

Here's another example you can take the writer though:

- Insomnia looks like … a black night.
- Insomnia smells like … hot milk.
- Insomnia feels like … a hive in the brain.
- Insomnia tastes like … a bitter cherry.
- Insomnia sounds like … a car alarm going off without end.

The first three sense descriptions are fairly literal: Insomnia occurs in the night, hot milk helps us sleep, insomnia often occurs despite fatigue, which can feel like a hive behind the eyes. But the taste description is associative only in that it's negative. The sound description is closer to being literal—car alarms keep us up—but is less literal than the first three entries. To me, the comparison seems to refer less to the fact that car alarms keep us up and more to their repeated, hammering sound. This is to say: No need to be literal. No need to justify why the word in question sounds, smells, or tastes the way it does to the writer. The less literal, the better, in fact:

- Insomnia looks like … an inkblot.
- Insomnia smells like … a bouquet of poisonous mushrooms.
- Insomnia feels like … a dry hand.
- Insomnia tastes like … a bitter leaf.
- Insomnia sounds like … a leaking faucet.

You'll agree that all these comparisons evoke something negative, frightening, frustrating. They don't summon what insomnia is so much as what insomnia feels like. There's a useful lesson about poetry here: **It doesn't aim to define things; it aims to render an _experience_ of them.** (And only one person's experience.) There are lots of experiences of insomnia; all are equally valid and interesting for poets. That isn't to say that we should put down the first random sense associations that come to our minds (floor wax! bananas!). We need to sit with the word and wait to realize how it feels to us. It's a nebulous art, and it's hard to explain in rational terms because, in a sense, it's the opposite of rational. It's intuitive.

As for the poem-writing portion, the logic is similar to previous weeks. The writer has a ton of information—word associations, five-senses comparisons, the literal meaning itself, etc.—from which to choose a focus for a poem about the word in question. Again, the number of lines or stanzas doesn't matter. On the next page is a stab at a brief poem about insomnia:

Insomnia, you ancient dog.
By my bed every night,
Immobile, unleaving, a pile of flesh,
even when I send you away.

I throw the newspaper, the ball, the bone.
But your loyalty to me
Goes against even
Animal instinct.

You stay put, studying me with pitiful eyes,
As loving as death.

How did I come up with this poem? It has a lot to do with the word's actual meaning—it's about insomnia—but I hope you'll find that it's also infused with the feeling of insomnia: an old enemy, so old as to seem familiar, almost a friend, a nightly visitor more loyal than most things in life, loyal even when we wish that it wasn't. And so the poem tries to capture this combined sense of familiarity and frustration, love and hate, animating insomnia as an old dog, equal parts loyal and animalistically unrelenting.

SUBSTITUTION!

Here are the lines the student is to find substitutions for:

1. Insomnia, you _____ dog.
2. By my bed every night,
3. _____, _____, _____,
4. even when I _____ you away.
5. I throw the newspaper, the ball, the bone.
6. But your loyalty to me
7. Goes against even
8. Animal instinct
9. You stay put, studying me with _____ eyes,
10. As loving as _____.

Here are some options for the substitutions:

1. "old": sick, wasted, imperial, sentimental
3a, 3b. "immobile, collapsed": motionless, unmoving
3c. "pile of flesh": heap/mound/hill of fur/lead/ruin
4. "send": push, command, order
9. "pitiful": laughing, crying, gleaming, sad, morose, melancholy
10. "as death": as the hold of a viper/as a hand pushing me underground/as an airless room.

On the next page, I show how I chose those words:

Line 1: If insomnia is like a guard dog that won't release its owner into sleep, then that dog can be vicious, or bashful about having to keep this prisoner hostage, or unable to help its own role. That's the feeling that I get from the situation in the poem. So the adjectives I chose try to reflect that, though only "wasted" comes close in meaning to "old."

Line 3a, 3b: Self-explanatory, though note that I tried to choose words of a similar length. "Still" also means "immobile" but it messes up the rhythm of the line.

Line 3c: Self-explanatory, though notice that that the three alternatives for "flesh" gradually depart from literal equivalence, just as my substitutes in line 1 do.

Line 4: Self-explanatory.

Line 9: Variations based on the personality characteristics discussed in line 1.

Line 10: I decided to stick with the suffocation theme.

If the writer is stuck, put the poem aside for a moment and do a brainstorming/association exercise. Have the writer *draw* the dog in question, if she can draw, or ask her to come up with 10 characteristics for the dog—the color of its fur, the expression on its face, its posture, etc. (A character exercise of sorts.) For some of the adjectives, ask the writer to come up with a handful of words/feelings/images/etc. that pop into mind when that word is said aloud. Lurking among these associations is the answer the writer is looking for. (Of course, the writer can always check a thesaurus, but they're of limited use here. We're not practicing synonyms so much as looking for sharper alternatives, which could still be very effective despite meaning something slightly different.)

We'll talk more about revision in the future, but the basic idea is that there's no way we can write our best poem on the first try. "I don't revise" is a favorite defense of many young writers, probably because they think there's something natural about a first draft: If you start tinkering with the results of that original rush of inspiration, you're going to mess it all up. But I would say the reverse is true when it comes to revision. After you've used your intuition to get the first draft out, you need to reactivate your mind for a closer look at the second draft, to see whether your instincts have given you the best possible results. The first draft will always have vigor, vitality, a creative messiness. And some of its rough edges may be worth preserving. But only a calm, rational mind can decide that. The job of the second draft isn't to take the bite out of the first. It's to sand down the rough edges a little, to say the same things more effectively. The first draft's aim is just to get the material down. The second's, freed from the challenge of having to fill a blank page, can focus on quality. It's easier to revise than to write, but it's just as important.

FILL IN THE BLANK / POETIC MAD LIBS

Remind the writer that he doesn't have to guess the "accurate" meaning of the line/stanza. It's perfectly fine to change the meaning with the new word choice.

However, you can begin by asking: "What do you think is the meaning here?" Whether the writer is able to answer or not, follow up by asking what *feeling* he gets from the words. Together, jot down five words that come to mind in response to that question. Then, come up with word associations for one or several of the words. Finally, ask the student whether the blank spot is asking for a noun, adjective, verb, etc. After coming up with a plausible replacement—say, a noun—ask the writer if another sentence part might work. (Verb, adjective, etc.) It's okay—and worth it—to rearrange the syntax a little to make another sentence part work. For blanks that seem to ask for a rhyme, make sure at least one of the writer's fill-in-the-blanks rhymes, but one does not. Doing both will demonstrate how much rhyme changes sound. When all else fails, try the thesaurus!

KENNING

Here are some possible kennings for the 10 originals:

1. Book—brain food
2. Computer—mind substitute
3. Wall—house borders
4. Wind—God's breath
5. Clothing—human leaves
6. Spaceship—frontier pioneer
7. Leaves—a tree's beard
8. Smile—the face's sun
9. Aggression—heart monsoon
10. Congress—law house

I tried to break down the original into its component parts. What is a book? The word is so ubiquitous, the image of a book so easily called up by the word, that it takes an effort to remember that "book" isn't the object's most basic denominator (few words truly are): At its simplest, "book" refers to a bunch of ink on a page. But a kenning is often more imaginative than that, so I kept thinking, expanding the definition to include the book's role and purpose in our world. That's how I came up with "brain food."

If the writer is struggling, ask:

• What is it?
• What function does it serve?
• What would we do without it?

The 5 Senses can be useful here, too:

- What does it look like?
- What does it smell like?
- What does it taste like?
- What does it sound like?
- What does it feel like?

RHYME REDUX

If the writer decides to do the poem I've provided: It's too overwhelming, before start-ing, to try to come up with some idea that could potentially suit all the end-words. Don't worry about lines 3–14. Have her focus on the end of line 1, with one eye half-open toward the end of line 2. What might make sense if the lines have to end with "still" (line 1) and "will" (line 2)?

"Still" can work as an adjective (as in "be still"), verb ("still that noise"), or adverb ("still unfinished"). It's a pretty versatile word. What about "will"? Also many meanings: verb of many uses ("will make," "will himself"), noun ("will of a dying man"), etc. This kind of brain-jog can help before trying to come up with a two-liner that incorporates both.

When trying to come up with two lines that might work, advise the writer, at first, not to worry about making sure each of the lines ends in the right word. Just find a phrase that can incorporate both, wherever they fall:

> In the still gaze of the moon, the will rises like a sleepwalker.

In your next attempt, see if you can sneak at least one of the words toward the end of its line:

> I will this screaming child:
> Be still.

Keep playing until you arrive at something that works:

> The rising moon's still
> gaze awakes the will.

For the assignment to write a poem of rhymes from scratch, have the writer go back to this level's first section. (What to write about?) However, it isn't necessary to choose a subject before you start to rhyme. The Ron Carlson method from Week 3 of the fiction section can work in poetry, too. Have the student jot down a first line—it can be anything, practically anything, say ...

> "Say anything, practically anything."

Okay—we've got a first line and will now shift our attention to coming up with a second that obeys the rhyme scheme. That's as far as the writer has to think at this point.

If the second line has to rhyme with the first, the writer can brainstorm some rhymes for "anything" on a separate sheet of paper: "everything," "swing" (a kind of near-rhyme because the accent is on the final/only syllable), "if it stings," "posturing." One will most likely lead to an idea for the second line:

> Instead of all this silent posturing.

And so on, using this method.

If the writer is struggling to write a poem and rhyme at the same time—which would be understandable—here are two modified versions of this exercise:

1. Have the writer write a 14-line poem without trying to rhyme. Then, a rough draft of the product available, have her start tinkering with the language until some rhymes emerge, as per the above guidance.
2. Use an already-written poem, and focus only on tweaking it to rhyme. Both Walt Whitman and Robert Frost are good for unrhymed poetry, though most contemporary poetry doesn't rhyme as well. The websites of *The New Yorker*, *The Paris Review*, and Poets.org should give you plenty of options.

REPETITION

As usual, the first step is the hardest. Tell the writer not to worry about what comes after the first and second line. It's also fine to get a leg up by roping in other family members. "Hey, Dad: How would you finish a line that starts, 'If I could…'?" When Dad says, "If I could take a nap right now, I would," the writer has something to run with. The second line might respond to the first, either humorously ("If I could make sure no one noticed") or not ("If I could shed twenty years and twenty pounds, I would.") Ending every line with "I would" creates an interesting double-echo, and in fact fulfills this week's other assignment in one go.

Speaking of that other version, you can brainstorm the same way. If the writer has chosen a general-enough word, you might start by asking him to write several sentences that end in that word and make sense. For instance, for "light," he might start by enumerating the various meanings the word can take. Then use those meanings to write sentences:

- After night, there's always light.
- I ask you, sir, Do you see the light?
- My soul is heavy, my body light.

In modified form, these can lead to a poem:

> My soul is heavy, my body light,
> After I have closed the light.
> In the dark a man asks, Sir, do you see the light?
> Only after night do I see the light.

LINE BREAKS

If the writer doesn't know how to begin, dispense with the assignment's limitations. Ask him to compose a line of poetry or to take one from an existing poem and divide it into 16 one-word lines. Have him do this several times to get the feel of the pattern, and make sure to read each example out loud, pausing at the end of each line. Discuss how differently the line in question sounds in the original vs. the one-word-per-line pattern. Which one is more suspenseful? On a scale of 1–10, ask the writer to rank the "speed" of the original vs. the one-word-per-line version. Ask the writer to come up with five words of description for the feeling elicited by each. Ask him whether the naturally rushing form of the one-word-per-line agrees with the meaning of the words in question.

After this prepwork, the writer should be ready to try to come up with a new one from scratch. Once he does, ask the same questions: Suspenseful? Speed? Feelings elicited? And so on.

INTRODUCTION TO METER—THE HAIKU

The writer is having to juggle two assignments at once here: Coming up with a poem and confining it to an assigned number of syllables. One way to organize these challenges is to delay the second. First, have the writer compose a three-line poem—of however many syllables per line—on the assigned subject. You might be surprised by how close the result might come to the assigned number of syllables. When we don't have to worry about the assignment officially, we tend to do a pretty good job of fulfilling it, anyway.

Even if the syllables are off, at least the writer has something to work with. Ask him to:

- Come up with several other ways of saying the same thing.
- Come up with several synonyms for each of the key words.
- Shuffle the lines. (That is, Line 1 gets tried out as both Line 2 and Line 3. Line 2 also gets tried out in both other positions. Same for Line 3.) For a great source on how many different ways the same idea can be phrased, check out this site: bopsecrets.org/gateway/passages/basho-frog.htm It offers 30 translations of Basho's frog-jumping-in-the-water haiku.

The writer might ask why we restrict ourselves through form in this way. Why not free ourselves to use all the tools at our disposal to write the best poem we can? It's a fair question, and a tough one to answer to a teenager who is overly familiar with the negative side of restriction—house rules, curfew, chores, etc.

Restrictions challenge us to write an even better poem than we would have without them because the poem has to obey all the restrictions of form while also being as excellent as a poem without restrictions. It's the equivalent of the one-armed push-up: Far fewer people can do that, but it makes them a lot stronger than those who can manage only a two-armed. Why do boxers training for a bout subject themselves to all sorts of restrictions (blindfolds, running with weights, etc.)? It's to exercise their strength and instincts in a way they wouldn't have been able to otherwise. Limitations force us to work harder than we would have to if they didn't exist. And as you, the mentor, can surely attest, they aren't a bad reminder, generally speaking, of how the world works.

A LECTURE ABOUT SOUND

If at this point, the writer develops nothing more than an ear for the basic idea that there are soft and hard sounds, and that each group broadcasts a different feeling, that would be fine. The more exacting nuances of sound can wait for the next two levels of this series.

Do remind the student that no poet sits down intending to make a poem sound "hard" or "soft" or something else. Rather, a poet is generally aware of the sound of words. To a poet, "dock" is hard, and if he intends to write a poem about an idyllic day on the lake, he will use this word carefully. Even words that share a lot of similar sounds have different personalities in different contexts. "Fortress" is hard, not least because of what it means. "Effervescence"—which also features "f"s, "r"s, and "s"s aplenty—has a different effect. A poet who isn't conscious of these differences, who writes a poem about an idyllic day on the lake full of "dock" and "beak" and "deep" and "bat" is writing an unwittingly dark poem. (If this disagreement between sound and meaning is *intentional*, it can be powerful. If it's accidental, if the "bats smack the sweet night air/ with black wings, circling the deep," the hard feel of "bats," "smack," "night," "black," "wings," and "deep" is going to create a far more powerful effect than the meaning (and sound) of "sweet" and "air," and make the reader think the poet doesn't know what he's doing.

SOUND PERSONALITIES

The best thing you can do for the writer in this exercise is to explain the concept of playing around. Poetry isn't as goal-oriented as a math problem. Of course, every poet wants to write a beautiful poem, but it isn't as simple as sitting down, drawing a long breath, and getting down to it. Ideas are wily things; they don't come consistently or linearly. And just as a boxer needs to spend time jumping rope and punching sandbags in order to prepare for the real deal in the ring, the writer benefits from wordplay exercises of this sort.

The toughest challenge here is likely to be how to go from the unfamiliar word to an association. What's "correct"? Even if the writer knows that "correct" isn't the goal here, how to arrive at some associations? With an unknown word, the mind tends to draw a blank. One way to do this is to grab a handful of sentences—from the newspaper, from the radio, from a book—and write them out on a piece of paper. Then scratch out the relevant sentence part (noun, verb, adjective) in each sentence and replace with the writer's version of my "prolegomena." Does any one of the sentences read better for one reason or another? Maybe "better" simply means "funny," or maybe it means that the word fits elegantly for one reason or another. You and the writer will feel it right away on reading the sentence. For instance, take this sentence, from a 2006 article about food in the French city of Nice: "In the southern part of the area you get a sense of the nearby sea, but can only glimpse it through a couple of arches in the wall." Playing around with "prolegomena" gives us several options:

1. "In the southern part of the *prolegomena* you get a sense of the nearby sea, but can only glimpse it through a couple of arches in the wall."
2. "In the southern part of the area you get a sense of the nearby *prolegomena*, but can only glimpse it through a couple of arches in the wall."
3. "In the southern part of the area you get a sense of the nearby sea, but can only glimpse the *prolegomena* through a couple of arches in the wall."
4. "In the southern part of the area you get a sense of the nearby sea, but can only glimpse it through a couple of *prolegomena* in the wall."
5. "In the southern part of the area you get a sense of the nearby sea, but can only glimpse it through a couple of arches in the *prolegomena*."

To me, the first, fourth, and fifth sentences read as if the author really meant to use the word "prolegomena"! As I've mentioned, there's something vaguely Greek about the word to me, so when you throw in "southern" and "arches," it almost seems to belong.

In the second sentence, the word reads as if it refers to an oddity of some kind. I feel something similar in the third sentence.

What about the sound of the sentence? To me, the hard g in "prolegomena" stands out. It echoes the hard g in "get" and "glimpse." The proximity of the "p" and "l" in "prolegomena" connects to the proximity of the same letters in "couple." But "prolegomena" also stands out, like a rock outcropping in a sea, in this sentence, because there are many sounds it doesn't connect to: All the "s" sounds in this sentence—"southern," "sense," "sea," "glimpse"—as well as the c, r, and w in "couple," "arches," "wall."

What you've just done is come up with a soundscape for the word "prolegomena." Does it lead us to anywhere in particular? No. We're just playing. In poetry, the journey is sometimes as useful as the destination.

STOP BEING SO RATIONAL!

You can help the writer by encouraging him to feel unselfconscious about writing down dreams. Reassure him that he can keep certain things private if he wishes, but just as critically, remind him that his dream-diary jottings don't have to make sense, that this should be seen as an opportunity for play rather than as a consignment to a frightening lack of meaning. We live in such a meaning-focused society that our first instinct with the unfamiliar is to become put off, and, consequently, to wall ourselves off. But if we can manage to remain open to, and unthreatened by, the foreign, wonderful and unexpected things will emerge.

How to go from a week's worth of observations to a poem? There are many potential subjects here:

- The writer can write about something he's learned about dreaming in general, by virtue of paying closer attention to it.
- The writer can write about a single dream, or fragment of a dream, fleshing it out in more detail, imagining a prequel or sequel to it, so to speak.
- The writer can pick a single image, or even a word, and riff on that, never mentioning dreaming at all.
- Even if the writer attempts to impose semantic (meaning-related) "sense" on the images, they are likely to be so disparate that this is likely to result in something wonderfully fanciful and absurd.

Finally, try to firm up for the writer the notion that dreams are useful for poetry because they obey a nonrational flow. That is, they take material from the brain, but reorganize it according to the dictates of the subconscious rather than the conscious. The subconscious has a lot more to do with feeling and intuition than reason and sense; poetry springs partly from the same source.

Remind the student, as well, that he doesn't have to "understand" the dream. "Why was I on a schoolbus? I don't go to school. Is it because I wish I did?" This line of questioning may be fruitful for the student's own understanding of himself, but this attempt to "understand" the dream isn't useful for poetry. Boiling a dream down to its rational meaning is for psychology class; in art, it sounds wooden rather than mystical. The poetic understanding of the dream comes through the writing out of sensations about it. This is a vague concept, I know, but it will be far less vague by the end of this series.

Finally: We are transitioning from meaning-related assignments to nonsense-related assignments where words and ideas appeal to us not because we understand them, but because of the sound they create or the feelings they inspire. Next week's assignment will take this notion even further by asking the student to come up with a dozen nonsense comparisons, like "yellow ponies" and "the chimney of the sun" and "lamp like a raptor."

ANTI-COMPARISONS

If the writer is having trouble coming up with source things/objects/feelings, point them to the living room; have them open the refrigerator; ask them their mood when they woke up. (The couch is a dragon/is rain/is a decision. The milk is a mantis/a fryer/a rooster. Grogginess is a deer antler/a stuffed deer head/is a pair of long johns.)

Here are some other possibilities:

- Stove
- Curtain
- Scooter
- Cherry orchard
- Desert

- Whiner
- Church service
- Ice cream
- Airplane pilot
- Letter opener

- Stingy person
- Clock
- Train platform
- Crying
- Revenge

If the writer can't help coming up with overly "sensible" comparisons, draw up a checklist filled with categories drawn from the Five Senses:

- Shape
- Sound
- Touch
- Taste
- Look

Another way to get the writer to go against sense is to ask him "What is it not like?" and then have that be the answer.

Still another approach is to find a foreign word—open up amazon.fr or the Hungarian version of Wikipedia—and ask the writer to compare "voiture" and "ittassag" to something in English. Then translate the foreign word using an online translator. No chance of being held too closely by "correct" meaning here.

I'M A POET AND I DON'T KNOW [WHAT THE WORD MEANS]

Start by helping the writer choose 16 unknown words. (I'd flip through a dictionary—a piece of paper covering the side with the definitions until she stumbles on 16 she doesn't know. If you want to make sure she doesn't see the definitions, you flip and call out words to her, asking if she knows them or can guess.) I had to turn many away because I had a vague idea of what they meant or could guess from a root or suffix.

As in the past, advise the student not to worry about too much past the first line. In fact, you could pick it out of the newspaper, if you'd like, subbing the first unknown word for one in the newspaper sentence. The tilt of that line will suggest a (broad) narrative for the remainder. If the student is stuck, take a line from another article in the newspaper. (Repeat as necessary.) There's no way the line can be wrong! The most important thing is for the writer to have fun. This exercise is all about play and sense-lessness (albeit of a kind that can teach us a lot about poetry).

WRITE A POEM

Just as in last year's final exercise, don't lean overmuch on the writer this week. To decide what kind of poem she'd like to write and how, she may wish to revisit some of this year's lessons—suggest this because it will actually give her ideas; coming up with something off the top of one's head is harder—but it's optional.

Depending on what kind of poem the writer decided to try, you may wish to steer and critique as per that lesson's mentor guidance, but it may be fun—and useful, too—to let the writer feel like she's completely on her own, answering only to herself or himself.